Second edition

VSAM
for the
COBOL
Programmer

Mike Murach & Associates, Inc.
2560 West Shaw Lane, Suite 101
Fresno, California 93711-2765
(209) 275-3335

Second edition

VSAM for the COBOL Programmer

Concepts ■ COBOL ■ JCL ■ IDCAMS

Doug Lowe

Editors

Sheila Lynch
Tim Schaldach

Graphics designer/ Desktop publisher

Steve Ehlers

Related products

VSAM: Access Method Services and Application Programming by Doug Lowe

MVS JCL by Doug Lowe
MVS TSO, Part 1 and Part 2 by Doug Lowe

DOS/VSE JCL (Second Edition) by Steve Eckols and Michele Milnes
DOS/VSE ICCF by Steve Eckols

VM/CMS: Commands and Concepts by Steve Eckols
VM/CMS: XEDIT Commands and Features by Steve Eckols

How to Design and Develop COBOL Programs by Paul Noll and Mike Murach
The COBOL Programmer's Handbook by Paul Noll and Mike Murach

Structured ANS COBOL, Part 1 and Part 2 by Mike Murach and Paul Noll
Report Writer by Steve Eckols
VS COBOL II (Second Edition) by Anne Prince

CICS for the COBOL Programmer, Part 1 and Part 2 by Doug Lowe
DB2 for the COBOL Programmer, Part 1 and Part 2 by Steve Eckols
IMS for the COBOL Programmer, Part 1 and Part 2 by Steve Eckols

© 1989 Mike Murach & Associates, Inc.
All rights reserved.
Printed in the United States of America.
20 19 18 17 16 15 14 13 12 11 10 9 8 7 6

Library of Congress Cataloging-in-Publication Data

Lowe, Doug.
    VSAM for the COBOL programmer.

    Includes index.
    1. COBOL (Computer program language)   2. Virtual
computer systems.   I. Title.
QA76.73.C25L69   1989   005.2′ 25   88-60035
ISBN 0-911625-45-3

Contents

Preface

This book is a revision of our 1982 book, *VSAM for the COBOL Programmer*. The first edition was used in many colleges and junior colleges for classroom instruction, and it was used in hundreds of businesses for in-house training. This edition is a thoroughly revised and improved version of the first edition.

What this book does

Like the first edition, this book presents everything you need to know for writing COBOL programs that process VSAM files on an IBM mainframe. That's what makes this book unique. You can find everything you need for VSAM file handling in a single book.

In section 1, this book presents all of the VSAM concepts and terminology you need to know for COBOL programming. In section 2, it presents all of the COBOL elements you need to know. In chapter 5 of section 3, it shows you how to code MVS and VSE JCL for running COBOL programs that process VSAM files. And in chapter 6 of section 3, it shows you how to use the Access Method Services program (also know as AMS or IDCAMS) for setting up and processing VSAM files.

Although this book presents everything an applications programmer needs to know for VSAM file handling, I've deliberately omitted those features of VSAM that a programmer doesn't need to know. For instance, I have omitted performance, recovery, and security considerations because applications programmers usually don't have to deal with them. In general, those details are handled by systems programmers.

To make it easy for you to learn COBOL for VSAM files, this book includes the specifications, structure charts, and COBOL listings for nine complete programs. These programs show you how to code most of the VSAM file handling functions that you'll ever need to use: file loading, sequential and random updating by primary key, random updating by alternate key, and so on. After you've used these programs to help you learn the COBOL elements for VSAM files, you can use them for reference as you write your own VSAM programs.

In short, this book presents everything a COBOL programmer needs to know about VSAM. And after you've used it for training, it becomes an excellent reference. With this book in hand, you should rarely have to consult an IBM manual as you develop COBOL programs that process VSAM files.

Who this book is for

This book is intended for COBOL programmers who haven't yet mastered VSAM file handling. This includes experienced programmers who have never worked on IBM mainframes so they haven't had any experience with VSAM. This includes less experienced programmers who want to improve their capabilities for handling VSAM files. And this includes programmer trainees who haven't learned how to write COBOL programs that process indexed or relative files. The only assumption this book makes is that the readers know how to write batch COBOL programs that process sequential files.

How the second edition improves upon the first

If you've read the first edition, you'll quickly see that the second edition of *VSAM for the COBOL Programmer* is a major improvement for several reasons. Naturally, I improved upon the organization and illustrative material of the first edition. But I also made some important additions to the contents.

First, I corrected the most obvious omissions of the first edition by adding material on using dynamic access and alternate keys. You'll probably use sequential and random access more than dynamic access. And you'll probably process key-sequenced files by primary key rather than by an alternate key. But both of these features are worth knowing about.

Second, this edition presents the VSAM file handling elements for IBM's VS COBOL II compiler, as well as for the VS COBOL compiler. If you haven't already converted to COBOL II and you work on an MVS or CMS system, you probably will some day. So this material will help prepare you for the change. On the other hand, VS COBOL II isn't available on VSE systems, so I've put all of the COBOL II elements in a separate topic that VSE users can skip.

Finally, this edition presents more information on the Access Method Services (AMS) program than the first edition did. I did this partly because our readers asked for it and partly because I realized that the typical COBOL programmer needs to know more about AMS than I presented in the first edition. In its expanded state, you shouldn't ever have to consult an AMS manual as you develop COBOL programs.

Related books

Since this book combines information from several of our other books, you may want to know more about them. Also, if you want to know more about VSAM, operating systems, structured programming, or COBOL, you may be interested in one or more of the related books.

If you want to learn more about VSAM, we offer my other VSAM book, which is called *VSAM: Access Method Services and Application Programming*. This book presents AMS more from the point of view of a systems programmer than an applications programmer. As a result, it shows you how to use the performance, recovery, and security features of AMS. In addition, it shows you how to process VSAM files using assembler language and CICS as well as COBOL. So if you want to know more about VSAM, this is the book to get.

If you want to learn more about the operating system you're using we have a variety of offerings. For MVS systems, we offer three books that I wrote: *MVS JCL* and *Part 1* and *Part 2* of *MVS TSO*. For VSE systems, we offer two books by Steve Eckols: *DOS/VSE JCL* and *DOS/VSE ICCF*. And for VM/CMS systems, we offer two books: one on concepts and commands and one on XEDIT.

Perhaps the most important book we've ever done for COBOL programmers is called *How to Design and Develop COBOL Programs*. It shows experienced COBOL programmers how to design, code, and test programs that are easy to debug and maintain. And it shows them how to increase their productivity, often by 200 percent or more. As an accompanying reference, we offer *The COBOL Programmer's Handbook*. These books present the design and coding principles that I used when I developed the programming examples in *VSAM for the COBOL Programmer*.

Last, if you want to improve your COBOL capabilities, we offer books that will help you complete your training. Our two part series on *Structured ANS COBOL* will teach you everything you need to know about COBOL for batch programs. Our *Report Writer* book will show you how to use the Report Writer feature of COBOL, and our *VS COBOL II* book will show you how to use all of the language of the VS COBOL II compiler. Finally, our two part courses on *CICS for the COBOL Programmer*, *DB2 for the COBOL Programmer*, and *IMS for the COBOL Programmer* will teach you everything you need to know about CICS, DB2, and IMS programming in COBOL.

Conclusion

I hope you enjoy using this book as you learn to write COBOL programs for VSAM file handling. After you've used it to master file handling, I hope it becomes a useful reference for you.

If you have any comments or questions, I welcome them. If you check the last few pages of this book, you'll find a postage-paid comment form. You'll also find a postage-paid order form in case you want to order any of the related products. I thank you for reading this book.

Doug Lowe
Fresno, California
April 19, 1989

An introduction to VSAM

The one chapter in this section presents the background information you need before you can learn how to develop COBOL programs that process VSAM files. If you're already familiar with VSAM, this information may be review for you. But even if it is, I recommend that you skim this chapter to make sure you're familiar with its concepts and terms. Because they're used throughout this book, you should make sure you understand them before you continue.

Chapter 1

VSAM concepts

On IBM mainframe systems, file processing is handled by special components of the operating system called *access methods*. *VSAM*, which stands for the *Virtual Storage Access Method*, was developed in the mid-1970s as a replacement for some of the older, less efficient access methods. Today, VSAM is the most widely used access method on IBM mainframes. One of its strengths is that it is essentially the same no matter which operating system you use, DOS/VSE or MVS.

In this chapter, I'll start by introducing you to the three types of files that are supported by VSAM. Next, I'll explain how VSAM manages the records within a file and how VSAM uses catalogs to keep track of files. Then, I'll introduce you to the JCL requirements for VSAM files. I'll finish by introducing the Access Method Services program that you'll use for performing utility functions on VSAM files.

The three types of VSAM files

Although VSAM is just one access method, it provides for three types of files. These file types correspond directly to the three types of files supported by COBOL in the 1974 and the 1985 standards: sequential files, indexed files, and relative files. Under VSAM, though, these files are referred to as entry-sequenced data sets, key-sequenced data sets, and relative record data sets.

Before I describe each type of file in more detail, I want you to realize that you can use three different terms to refer to a VSAM file. In addition to the terms *file* and *data set*, which you are probably familiar

Disk Location	Employee number	First name	Middle Initial	Last name	Social security number
1	01001	Stanley	L	Harris	499-35-5069
2	01002	Thomas	T	Bluestone	213-64-9290
3	01003	William	J	Collins	279-64-1210
4	01004	Alice		Westbrook	899-16-9235
5	01005	Constance	M	Abbott	334-96-8721
6	01007	Jean	B	Glenning	572-68-3100
7	01008	Paul	M	Collins	703-47-5748
8	01009	Marie	A	Littlejohn	558-12-6168
9	01010	E	R	Siebart	559-35-2479
10	01012	Ronald	W	Crawford	498-27-6117

Figure 1-1   An entry-sequenced data set that was created in employee number sequence

with, you can refer to a VSAM file as a *cluster*. For instance, you use a command called DEFINE CLUSTER to define a VSAM file.

Entry-sequenced data sets   An *entry-sequenced data set (ESDS)* is the simplest type of VSAM file. Its records are stored one after another in consecutive order, as illustrated by figure 1-1. When your program reads a record from an ESDS, VSAM gives it the record from the next physical location on the disk. When your program writes a record to an ESDS, VSAM writes it in the next physical location.

When you code your program in COBOL, you indicate this file type by specifying ORGANIZATION IS SEQUENTIAL in the SELECT statement. In chapter 3, you'll learn how to process a VSAM ESDS in COBOL.

Key-sequenced data sets   A *key-sequenced data set (KSDS)* is set up so you can access its records sequentially or randomly, depending on your processing requirements. To do that, the KSDS includes an *index component* that relates the value in a *key field* to the actual location of the record on the disk. Figure 1-2 shows how that works when the key field is employee number. By using the index component, your program can quickly access any record in a file without reading through the records themselves, which are in the *data component* of the file. And your program can process a KSDS sequentially almost as fast as it can process an ESDS.

When you code your program in COBOL, you indicate this file type by specifying ORGANIZATION IS INDEXED in the SELECT statement. Then, the ACCESS clause in the SELECT statement specifies

Index component		Data component					
Employee number	Disk Location	Disk Location	Employee number	First name	Middle Initial	Last name	Social security number
01001	9	1	01003	William	J	Collins	279-64-1210
01002	2	2	01002	Thomas	T	Bluestone	213-64-9290
01003	1	3	01007	Jean	B	Glenning	572-68-3100
01004	6	4	01008	Paul	M	Collins	703-47-5748
01005	5	5	01005	Constance	M	Abbott	334-96-8721
01007	3	6	01004	Alice		Westbrook	899-16-9235
01008	4	7	01009	Marie	A	Littlejohn	558-12-6168
01009	7	8	01012	Ronald	W	Crawford	498-27-6117
01010	10	9	01001	Stanley	L	Harris	499-35-5069
01012	8	10	01010	E	R	Siebart	559-35-2479

Figure 1-2   A key-sequenced data set that uses employee number as the key

whether your program will use sequential processing, random processing, or dynamic processing (a combination of the two). Because key-sequenced files are the most widely used VSAM files, you'll learn how to process them in COBOL in chapter 2, before you learn how to process entry-sequenced files.

Relative record data sets   A *relative record data set (RRDS)* lets you access each record at random without the overhead of maintaining an index. Instead, each record in an RRDS is numbered, starting with 1 for the first record. This is illustrated in figure 1-3. Then, to access a specific record in an RRDS, all you have to know is the *relative record number*. If, for example, you know the employee number of the record you're looking for in figure 1-3, you can subtract 1000 from it to get the relative record number. Note, however, that any routine that converts the value in a key field to a relative record number is likely to leave empty records within the file. Because there aren't any employee records with numbers 1006 and 1011 in figure 1-3, relative record numbers 6 and 11 are empty.

When you code your program in COBOL, you indicate this file type by specifying ORGANIZATION IS RELATIVE in the SELECT statement. However, relative record data sets are rarely used because it's usually too difficult to relate a key field in a record to a relative record number in a file and still make efficient use of the disk storage. Occa-

Relative record number	Employee number	First name	Middle Initial	Last name	Social security number
1	01001	Stanley	L	Harris	499-35-5069
2	01002	Thomas	T	Bluestone	213-64-9290
3	01003	William	J	Collins	279-64-1210
4	01004	Alice		Westbrook	899-16-9235
5	01005	Constance	M	Abbott	334-96-8721
6					
7	01007	Jean	B	Glenning	572-68-3100
8	01008	Paul	M	Collins	703-47-5748
9	01009	Marie	A	Littlejohn	558-12-6168
10	01010	E	R	Siebart	559-35-2479
11					
12	01012	Ronald	W	Crawford	498-27-6117

Figure 1-3   A relative record data set that has a simple relationship between employee number and relative record number

sionally, though, a relative record file can come in handy. That's why chapter 4 will show you how to process an RRDS in COBOL.

How VSAM manages the records in a file

Every VSAM file has a data component that contains the file's data records. In addition, as you saw in figure 1-2, every key-sequenced data set has an index component that contains the file's indexes. No matter what the file organization is, however, VSAM uses the same basic techniques to keep track of the records in the file. Although these techniques are complicated, you don't need to know much about them to write effective COBOL programs. All you need to understand are a couple of basic record management concepts.

To start, you need to understand that VSAM stores the logical records of a file in fixed-length blocks called *control intervals*. This is illustrated by figure 1-4. As you can see, each control interval usually contains more than one record. If, for example, your records are 1000 bytes long and the control intervals are 4096 bytes, each control interval can hold up to four records. If a record is larger than a control interval, VSAM can split the record across more than one control interval.

When a COBOL program reads a record from a VSAM file, VSAM reads an entire control interval into storage. Then, it extracts the record requested by the program and makes it available to the program. In other words, all physical I/O operations for VSAM files take place on

Control area 1

Control interval 1	Logical record 1	Logical record 2	Logical record 3
Control interval 2	Logical record 4	Logical record 5	Logical record 6
Control interval 3	Logical record 7	Logical record 8	Logical record 9
Control interval 4	Logical record 10	Logical record 11	Logical record 12
Control interval 5	Logical record 13	Logical record 14	Logical record 15
Control interval 6	Logical record 16	Logical record 17	Logical record 18

Control area 2

Control interval 7	Logical record 19	Logical record 20	Logical record 21
Control interval 8	Logical record 22	Logical record 23	Logical record 24
Control interval 9	Logical record 25	Logical record 26	Logical record 27
Control interval 10	Logical record 28	Logical record 29	Logical record 30
Control interval 11	Logical record 31	Logical record 32	Logical record 33
Control interval 12	Logical record 34	Logical record 35	Logical record 36

Figure 1-4   How records are grouped together in control intervals, and control intervals are grouped together in control areas

control intervals. As a result, the size of a file's control interval has a significant effect on the efficiency of the file's operations. Although the most efficient size depends on factors such as the file organization and the size of the file's records, a control interval size of 4096 bytes is efficient for most VSAM files.

Unlike COBOL, VSAM doesn't distinguish between files with fixed-length records and files with variable-length records. Since each control interval contains information that keeps track of the length of each record in the interval, VSAM doesn't know whether the record lengths are fixed or variable. When a file's records are all the same length, you can think of the records as fixed-length. But there's no real difference between fixed- and variable-length records in VSAM.

Besides keeping track of the number and size of the records in a control interval, VSAM keeps track of the amount of *free space* within each control interval. Depending on the file organization, you can use this free space to insert additional records in the control interval or to expand an existing record.

As you can see in figure 1-4, control intervals are grouped into *control areas*. When VSAM allocates disk space to a file, it allocates space in units of control areas. For most files, each control area occupies one cylinder of disk space (a *cylinder* consists of all the disk tracks that are under the disk's read/write heads at one time). Within each control area, free space can be distributed just as it can be distributed within control intervals. Since VSAM can use this free space for adding new records to a file or for expanding old records, this space gives VSAM some of its flexibility.

How VSAM catalogs keep track of the files on a system

To keep track of the files on a system, VSAM uses its catalog facility. Although each system can have just one VSAM *master catalog*, it can have an unlimited number of VSAM *user catalogs*. All user catalogs must be defined in the master catalog, and all VSAM files must be defined in the master catalog or in one of the user catalogs. These relationships are illustrated by figure 1-5. Notice here that non-VSAM files can also be cataloged in a VSAM catalog. Although this is common on MVS systems, it's unusual on DOS/VSE systems.

Although VSAM catalogs are similar under DOS/VSE and MVS, you should be aware of one difference. Under DOS/VSE, all VSAM files are stored in designated portions of disk volumes called *data spaces* (or just *spaces*). Within a data space, you can define more than one VSAM file. In addition, as files grow, VSAM can automatically assign additional space to the files from the free space remaining in the data space.

In contrast, MVS systems may or may not use data space to manage file allocations. Although older versions of MVS VSAM used data space, IBM introduced a new catalog management system in the mid-1980s. It is called the *Integrated Catalog Facility*, or *ICF*. Under ICF, you still have master and user catalogs, but the concept of VSAM data space has been dropped. As you'll see in chapter 6, though, this conceptual change

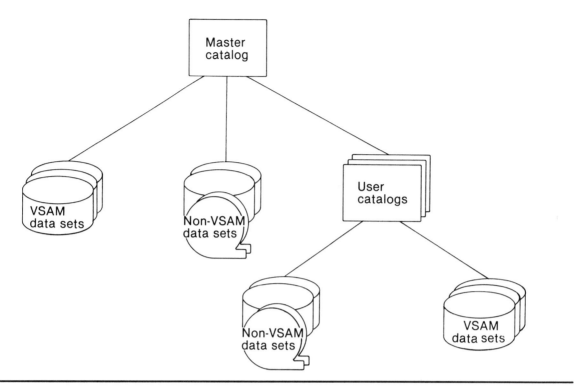

Figure 1-5   The relationships among the master catalog, user catalogs, and data sets

has only a trivial effect on the way you set up and use VSAM files on MVS systems.

The JCL for programs that process VSAM files

Because most of the information about a VSAM file is stored in its user catalog, coding the JCL for programs that process VSAM files is quite simple. This is true whether you're using DOS/VSE or MVS. In chapter 5, you'll learn how to code the JCL for VSAM files under either operating system.

AMS: The Access Method Services program

Your first direct contact with VSAM will probably be through its *Access Method Services* program, or *AMS*. Because IDC is the standard prefix for VSAM programs, you'll often hear this program referred to as *IDCAMS* (pronounced *id*-cams). You'll use this general-purpose program to create VSAM files; to copy, print, rename, or delete VSAM files; and to perform many other utility functions. In chapter 6, you'll learn how to use AMS to set up and process the VSAM files you'll use as you develop COBOL programs.

Discussion

In this chapter, I've tried to give you the minimum VSAM background you need for developing COBOL programs that process VSAM files. I hope you realize, though, that VSAM is far more complicated than this chapter indicates. However, for application programming in COBOL, you usually don't have to know any more about the internal workings of VSAM than this chapter presents.

Terminology

access method
VSAM
Virtual Storage Access Method
file
data set
cluster
entry-sequenced data set
ESDS
key-sequenced data set
KSDS
index component
key field
data component
relative-record data set
RRDS

relative record number
control interval
free space
control area
cylinder
master catalog
user catalog
data space
space
Integrated Catalog Facility
ICF
Access Method Services
AMS
IDCAMS

Objectives

1. List and describe the three kinds of VSAM files.

2. Explain the significance of a control interval or a control area.

3. Describe the functions of VSAM master and user catalogs.

4. Describe the functions of the AMS program.

The COBOL requirements for VSAM file handling

The three chapters in this section present the COBOL code for processing VSAM files. In these chapters, you'll learn how to code the language elements you need to access key-sequenced, entry-sequenced, and relative record data sets. Then, in section 3, you'll learn how to use JCL and the AMS program for your VSAM files.

Throughout this section, the figures and text present the language elements implemented by IBM's VS COBOL compiler. This compiler is based on the 1974 COBOL standards, and it runs on both MVS and VSE systems. With just a few exceptions, the VS COBOL statements are the same for both operating systems, but I'll point out any differences between MVS and VSE implementations as I go along.

In this section, I'll also present the language elements for file handling that are part of the 1985 COBOL standards. In particular, I'll present those elements that are already implemented or are going to be implemented by the VS COBOL II compiler. This compiler is the only 1985 COBOL compiler for IBM mainframes, and it only runs on MVS systems. To date, IBM hasn't announced a 1985 compiler for VSE systems, and no announcement is expected, so VSE users can ignore the 1985 COBOL elements.

Chapter 2

COBOL for key-sequenced data sets

Since most VSAM files are key-sequenced, it's essential that you master the concepts and techniques of this chapter. As you'll learn in the next two chapters, you may never have to use entry-sequenced or relative record data sets. But you're sure to use key-sequenced data sets.

Because the COBOL for key-sequenced data sets can be quite complex, this chapter is divided into five topics. Topic 1 presents some additional VSAM concepts for key-sequenced data sets, and topic 2 presents the COBOL elements you need for processing key-sequenced files with only one index. Then, since VSAM error processing is a complicated subject by itself, topic 3 shows you how to handle VSAM error conditions in COBOL. Next, topic 4 presents the COBOL elements you need for processing key-sequenced data sets with alternate indexes. Last, topic 5 presents the changes in processing key-sequenced data sets introduced by the 1985 COBOL standards and the VS COBOL II compiler.

Topic 1   VSAM concepts for key-sequenced data sets

As I explained in chapter 1, a VSAM *key-sequenced data set* (or *KSDS*) is a COBOL indexed file. A KSDS has a *data component* that stores the file's records and an *index component* that keeps track of each record's location in the data component. You can process a KSDS sequentially or randomly.

In this topic, I'll expand on the concepts I presented in chapter 1. First, I'll tell you more about the index component of a KSDS. Next, I'll tell you more about the free space within the data component of a KSDS. Last, I'll explain how alternate indexes are implemented by VSAM.

The index component of a KSDS

The index component of a KSDS has two parts: a sequence set and an index set. This is illustrated by figure 2-1. As you can see, the *sequence set* is the lowest level of the index component. It contains information that relates key values to specific control intervals in the data component of a file.

The *index set* of a KSDS can have one or more levels. The highest level of an index set always has just one record, and the records of the lowest level of the index set always contain pointers to sequence set records. This is illustrated by figure 2-1. In an index set with more than two levels, the top-level record points to the records at the next level, which in turn point to records at the next level, and so on, until the pointers reach the sequence set.

To understand how the KSDS index structure works, consider the simple file in figure 2-2. Here, the data component consists of three control areas, each with four control intervals. The numbers in the control intervals are the key values for the logical records. For example, the first control interval in control area 1 contains the three logical records whose key values are 012, 049, and 187.

For each control area in the data component of a KSDS, there is one record in the sequence set. As a result, the sequence set in figure 2-2 contains three records. Then, each sequence set record contains an *index entry* for each control interval in the corresponding control area. That index entry is the highest key value stored in the corresponding control interval. Notice that the sequence set records also contain *free pointers*, which I'll explain in a moment.

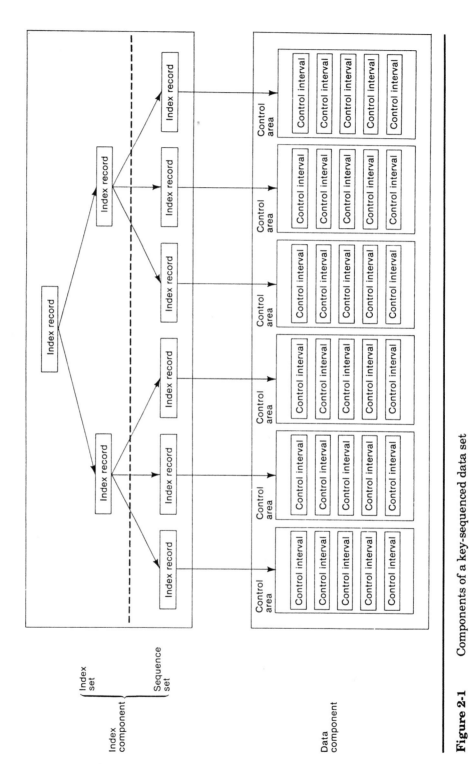

Figure 2-1 Components of a key-sequenced data set

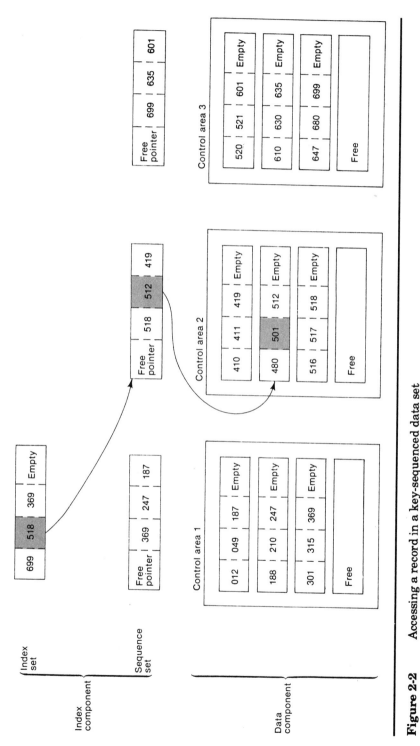

Figure 2-2 Accessing a record in a key-sequenced data set

The entries in the index set record in figure 2-2 contain the highest values stored in each of the sequence set records. Since a typical index set record is 512 bytes, which is enough for up to 58 sequence set records, many key-sequenced data sets require just one index set record. Since each sequence set record indexes a control area, which is typically a full cylinder, a single index set record provides for up to 58 cylinders of data. On a 3350 DASD volume, that's about 32 million bytes of data. If the file is larger than that, VSAM automatically creates additional index set records as needed, arranging them in levels like the ones in figure 2-1.

The arrows and the shading in figure 2-2 show the processing necessary to locate the record whose key value is 501. First, VSAM reads and searches the index set record to determine which sequence set record to use. Then, it reads and searches the correct sequence set record to determine which control interval to use. Finally, it reads and searches the control interval to locate the correct record.

Free space within the data component of a KSDS

A KSDS can have *free space* reserved within its data component to accommodate new records. You can reserve this space in two ways: (1) you can leave space within each control interval, and (2) you can leave entire control intervals empty. You make these specifications when you define a KSDS cluster using AMS.

Figure 2-3 shows the free space within a control area that consists of four control intervals. Three of the four control intervals contain four logical records and enough space for one more. The fourth control interval is empty. VSAM knows about this free space because each sequence set record in the index component contains a pointer to each free control interval in its associated control area. If you'll look back to figure 2-2, you'll see those free pointers. Although I omitted it from the figure, each control interval also contains control information that tells VSAM about the free space within that control interval.

Notice in figure 2-3 that within the control intervals, VSAM stores logical records in key sequence. When you add a record to a KSDS, VSAM inserts the record in its correct sequential location in the proper control interval and shifts the records that follow it in the control interval. If there isn't enough space in the control interval to hold the inserted record, VSAM performs a *control interval split* by moving some of the records in the control interval to one of the free control intervals. If there isn't a free control interval in the control area, VSAM performs a *control area split* by allocating a new control area, moving half of the control intervals from the original control area to the new one, and

Control area

Control interval 1

6011	6027	6030	6031	

Control interval 2

6040	6045	6052	6060	

Control interval 3

6068	6069	6071	6075	

Control interval 4

Figure 2-3   Free space distribution in the data component of a KSDS

performing a control interval split using one of the newly freed control intervals.

Alternate indexes

All indexed files have one *primary index*. However, an indexed file can also have one or more *alternate indexes*. An alternate index lets you access records by a field other than the *primary key* (or *base key*) field.

To understand the concept of an alternate index, consider figure 2-4. Here, the *base cluster* consists of the data component and the index component for the primary index. The records in the data component contain fields for employee name, employee number, and social security number. Since the file's base key is employee number, you can access the file directly by that field.

Besides this access by the primary key, you can use an alternate index to access the base cluster by social security number. As you can see in figure 2-4, VSAM lets you do this by relating each *alternate key* to a primary key. As the shading suggests, when you tell VSAM to retrieve the record for the employee with social security number 703-47-5748, VSAM first searches the alternate index for the alternate key. Then, it retrieves the related primary key (1008) and uses that value to locate the correct record in the base cluster.

In figure 2-4, each alternate key is associated with one primary key. This type of alternate key is called a *unique key*. In contrast, figure 2-5 shows an alternate index with *non-unique keys* (or *duplicate keys*). Here, the alternate key is last name.

To understand non-unique keys, consider the alternate index record for the last name Collins in figure 2-5. Here, the alternate key specifies two employee numbers: 1003 and 1008. When you process this alternate index sequentially, VSAM will retrieve both employee records in turn. However, when you process an alternate index file with duplicate keys randomly, VSAM retrieves only the first base cluster record for each alternate key. That's why you must use a combination of random and sequential processing to get all of the base cluster records by alternate key.

You may be interested to know that an alternate index is itself a key-sequenced data set. The index component of the alternate index points to records in the data component, just as in a standard KSDS. Then, each record in the alternate index's data component contains an alternate key value and one or more primary key values for the corresponding base cluster records.

It might surprise you to learn that VSAM doesn't necessarily *upgrade* every alternate index each time its base cluster changes. In fact, an alternate index is an *upgradable index* only if you use AMS to specify that VSAM should update it automatically whenever you make changes to the base cluster. Often, though, you won't specify alternate indexes as upgradable because this adds considerable overhead to alternate index processing. Most shops rebuild the alternate indexes periodically (usually, every night). If your shop does, you have to realize that the alternate indexes won't reflect additions or changes to your data sets until the next update.

Alternate index

Base cluster

		Index component			Data component					
Social security number	Employee number	Employee number	Disk Location	Disk Location	Employee number	First name	Middle Initial	Last name	Social security number
213-64-9290	01002	01001	1	1	01001	Stanley	L	Harris	499-35-5069
279-64-1210	01003	01002	2	2	01002	Thomas	T	Bluestone	213-64-9290
334-96-8721	01005	01003	3	3	01003	William	J	Collins	279-64-1210
498-27-6117	01012	01004	4	4	01004	Alice		Westbrook	899-16-9235
499-35-5069	01001	01005	5	5	01005	Constance	M	Abbott	334-96-8721
558-12-6168	01009	01007	6	6	01007	Jean	B	Glenning	572-68-3100
559-35-2479	01010	01008	7	7	01008	Paul	M	Collins	703-47-5748
572-68-3100	01007	01009	8	8	01009	Marie	A	Littlejohn	558-12-6168
703-47-5748	01008	01010	9	9	01010	E	R	Siebart	559-35-2479
899-16-9235	01004	01012	10	10	01012	Ronald	W	Crawford	498-27-6117

Figure 2-4   A KSDS with unique alternate keys

Base cluster

Alternate index

Last name	Employee number
Abbott	01005
Bluestone	01002
Collins	01003
	01008
Crawford	01012
Glenning	01007
Harris	01001
Littlejohn	01009
Siebart	01010
Westbrook	01004

Index component

Employee number	Disk Location
01001	1
01002	2
01003	3
01004	4
01005	5
01007	6
01008	7
01009	8
01010	9
01012	10

Data component

Disk Location	Employee number	First name	Middle Initial	Last name	Social security number
1	01001	Stanley	L	Harris	499-35-5069
2	01002	Thomas	T	Bluestone	213-64-9290
3	01003	William	J	Collins	279-64-1210
4	01004	Alice		Westbrook	899-16-9235
5	01005	Constance	M	Abbott	334-96-8721
6	01007	Jean	B	Glenning	572-68-3100
7	01008	Paul	M	Collins	703-47-5748
8	01009	Marie	A	Littlejohn	558-12-6168
9	01010	E	R	Siebart	559-35-2479
10	01012	Ronald	W	Crawford	498-27-6117

Figure 2-5 A KSDS with non-unique alternate keys

Discussion

This is perhaps more than you need to know about the VSAM concepts for key-sequenced data sets. I hope, however, that this conceptual background will help you as you write COBOL programs that process VSAM files. And I know this background will help you whenever you define a KSDS using AMS.

Terminology

key-sequenced data set	primary index
KSDS	alternate index
key field	primary key
data component	base key
index component	base cluster
sequence set	alternate key
index set	unique key
index entry	non-unique key
free pointer	duplicate key
free space	index upgrade
control interval split	upgradable index
control area split	

Objectives

1. Distinguish between an index set and a sequence set within the index component of a KSDS.

2. Explain how free space is used within the data component of a KSDS.

3. Explain how an alternate index for a KSDS works.

4. Distinguish between unique and non-unique keys within an alternate index.

Topic 2   COBOL for key-sequenced data sets with one index

This topic presents the COBOL elements for processing a VSAM key-sequenced file three ways: sequentially, randomly, and dynamically. When you use sequential processing, you access the records in key sequence. When you use random processing, you specify a key value for each access. And when you use dynamic processing, you can access records both sequentially and randomly. In this topic, I'll illustrate all three processing methods for files with just a primary index.

Sequential processing

When you process a KSDS sequentially, you access its records in the ascending order of the file's key field. You usually begin with the first record in the file and continue until the last.

Figure 2-6 summarizes the COBOL elements for processing VSAM key-sequenced files sequentially. After I discuss these COBOL elements, I'll illustrate them by presenting two programs: a sequential file-creation program and a sequential update program.

By the way, I have omitted the 1985 COBOL elements from figure 2-6. Since you can only use these elements if you have a VS COBOL II compiler, I'll cover them separately in topic 5.

The SELECT statement

The SELECT statement for an indexed file contains information about the file's name, organization, access mode, key field, and more. You must code a SELECT statement for each file you access from your COBOL program. The *file name* you specify in the first line of the SELECT statement is the name you use for the file throughout the program.

In the ASSIGN clause, you specify the file's *system name*. The system name isn't the name of the file. It's the name you use in your JCL when you want to refer to the file. Figure 2-7 presents the format for system names for both DOS/VSE and MVS systems. Although comments are allowed in both types of names, they're for compatibility with the system names in old programs. So, you usually don't code comments in the system names in new programs.

In the ORGANIZATION clause, you specify INDEXED. Then, you use the ACCESS clause to specify how you will process the file. Since

SELECT statement

```
SELECT file-name
    ASSIGN TO system-name
    ORGANIZATION IS INDEXED
    [ACCESS MODE IS SEQUENTIAL]
    RECORD KEY IS data-name-1
    [FILE STATUS IS data-name-2]
```

Note: The RECORD KEY field must be defined in the File Section as a field within the record description. And the FILE STATUS field must be defined in working storage as a two-byte alphanumeric item.

FD statement

```
FD  file-name
    LABEL RECORDS ARE STANDARD
    [RECORD CONTAINS integer CHARACTERS]
```

Procedure Division statements

```
     ⎧INPUT  file-name-1 ...⎫
OPEN ⎨OUTPUT file-name-2 ...⎬ ...
     ⎩I-O    file-name-3 ...⎭
```

```
                      ⎧EQUAL TO       ⎫
                      ⎪=              ⎪
START file-name [KEY IS⎨GREATER THAN  ⎬ data-name]
                      ⎪>              ⎪
                      ⎪NOT LESS THAN  ⎪
                      ⎩NOT <          ⎭

     [INVALID KEY imperative-statement]
```

```
READ file-name [NEXT] RECORD
    [INTO identifier]
    [AT END imperative-statement]
```

Figure 2-6   COBOL elements for sequential processing of key-sequenced files (part 1 of 2)

sequential processing is the default for the ACCESS clause, you can omit it when you want to process the file sequentially. I recommend you code it, though, because it's good documentation. The combination of the ORGANIZATION and ACCESS clauses makes it clear that although the file has indexed organization, you're going to access it sequentially.

```
WRITE record-name
    [FROM identifier]
    [INVALID KEY imperative-statement]


REWRITE record-name
    [FROM identifier]
    [INVALID KEY imperative-statement]


DELETE file-name RECORD
    [INVALID KEY imperative-statement]

CLOSE file-name ...
```

Figure 2-6   COBOL elements for sequential processing of key-sequenced files (part 2 of 2)

The RECORD KEY clause identifies the file's key field. During sequential processing, the indexed file's records are accessed in order based on this field. So you must code the RECORD KEY clause, and the key field you specify must appear in the file's record description in the File Section; it can't be a separate field in working storage. When you use the INTO and FROM options of the READ and WRITE statements, you usually define the entire record in the Working-Storage Section and just the key field in the File Section. You'll see this illustrated in the first sample program.

In the FILE STATUS clause, you identify one field that VSAM will use to provide information about each I/O operation for the file. It is a standard field the system updates every time you execute an I/O statement for the file. The value VSAM places in the field is called the *return code*. After an I/O statement has been executed, your program should examine this field to determine whether an error occurred. You must define this FILE STATUS field in working storage as a two-byte alphanumeric item.

Figure 2-8 lists the FILE STATUS codes you'll see most often when you process VSAM key-sequenced data sets. The first code, 00, indicates the operation was successful. The next code, 10, means you reached the end of the file. In other words, the AT END condition occurred. The next three codes are INVALID KEY conditions. Code 21 means a record was out of sequence during sequential processing. Code 22 means you tried to write a record with a duplicate key. And code 23 means you tried to access a record that doesn't exist. The last code, 24, indicates no more space was available for the file. You'll see how to use these codes in the

VS COBOL on a DOS/VSE system

Format: `SYSnnn-[comments-]name`

Example: `SYS020-INVMAST`

Notes: 1. The SYS number is a number between SYS000 and SYS240 that is used to identify a specific I/O device. Find out what numbers you should use on your system.

2. The *name* consists of from three to seven letters or digits, starting with a letter. For consistency, this can be the same name as the file name. This name is used in the JCL for running the program to relate the file description in the program with a file on disk.

VS COBOL or COBOL II on an MVS system

Format: `[comments-]ddname`

Example: `INVMAST`

Notes: The *ddname* is made up of eight or fewer letters or digits, starting with a letter. For consistency, this name can be the same as the file name. This name is used in the JCL for running the program to relate the file description in the program with a file on disk.

Figure 2-7   The formats of system names for key-sequenced files

sample programs in this topic. Then, in the next topic, you'll learn about some of the other, less common, return codes.

The FD statement

As you can see in figure 2-6, you code the FD statement for a KSDS using the LABEL RECORDS and RECORD CONTAINS clauses. All VSAM files have standard labels, so you always code the LABEL RECORDS clause just as it appears in figure 2-6.

The RECORD CONTAINS clause specifies the number of characters (bytes) in each record. Although this clause is optional, you should still code it since it's good documentation. It may also help you spot a coding problem. If the number of characters you specify in this clause doesn't agree with the number of bytes in the record description, you'll get a diagnostic during compilation.

FILE STATUS
code	Meaning
00	Successful completion
10	End of file reached
21	Sequence error
22	Duplicate key
23	Record not found
24	No more space

Figure 2-8   Common FILE STATUS codes for I/O operations on key-sequenced files

Procedure Division statements

The OPEN statement   The OPEN statement prepares a file for processing. It also specifies whether you will access the file for input only (INPUT), output only (OUTPUT), or both input and output (I-O).

The START statement   You use the START statement if you want to start sequential processing with a record other than the first record in the file. On the START statement, you specify the key of the record that sequential processing should start with. You can use the START statement with a file that's opened as INPUT or I-O. To use the START statement, move the key value of the first record to be processed to the file's RECORD KEY field. Then, issue the START statement.

As you can see in figure 2-6, the KEY clause is optional. If you omit it, the system looks for a record with a key equal to the key in the RECORD KEY field. If that record doesn't exist, an invalid key condition results with a file status code of 23. But usually, you'll want to start processing with the first record that's greater than or equal to a certain value. To do that, you use coding like this:

```
MOVE 1000 TO IM-ITEM-NO.
START INVMSTR
   KEY IS NOT < IM-ITEM-NO.
```

Here, processing will begin at the first record with a key value greater than or equal to 1000. If you don't use a START statement at all, processing will begin with the first record in the file.

The READ statement   When you open a file as INPUT or I-O, you use the READ statement to retrieve records in key sequence. Notice in figure 2-6 that you can code the word NEXT in the READ statement. But for sequential processing, you don't need it. In fact, I recommend you leave it out since it just means the READ statement will access the next record in sequence. And that's what the statement does anyway. However, as you'll see later in this topic, NEXT is required for a sequential READ statement when you use dynamic access.

The WRITE statement   To create a KSDS or to add records to one, you use the WRITE statement. You must first open the file as OUTPUT for file creation or as I-O for file additions.

The REWRITE statement   To execute a REWRITE statement for a key-sequenced data set, you must open it as I-O. The record you rewrite should be the last record you read from the file. In other words, you must read a record before you can rewrite it.

The DELETE statement   You can use the DELETE statement to remove records from a VSAM file you opened as I-O. The DELETE statement deletes the record read by the last READ statement. Under VSAM, the DELETE statement physically removes the record from the file, so the space is immediately available for a new record.

The CLOSE statement   In the CLOSE statement, you list the files you want to close. Just as you must open VSAM files at the beginning of each program, you must close them at the end.

Two sample programs

This section presents a file-creation program and a sequential update program. Although these programs are simpler than any production program would be, they illustrate the COBOL elements for processing VSAM indexed files sequentially. Both programs use the structured programming techniques we teach in our other COBOL books. But even if you're not familiar with structured programming, the program listings should be easy to follow.

I should point out here that since I ran these programs on a VSE system, the system names in the SELECT statements conform to VSE requirements. Other than that, the code is exactly the same for an MVS system.

A file-creation program   Figure 2-9 presents a program overview for a program that creates an inventory master KSDS from a file of sequential inventory records. Then, figure 2-10 presents the structure chart for this program. As you can see, the processing is quite simple. For each record in the sequential file, a record is written on the indexed file.

Program: INV1100 Create inventory file	Page: 1
Designer: Mike Murach	Date: 09-03-86

Input/output specifications

File	Description	Use
INVMAST	Sequential inventory master file	Input
INVMST1	Indexed inventory master file	Output

Process specifications

This program creates an indexed file of inventory master records from a
sequential file of master records. The records in the sequential file are
in sequence by item number, which is the key of the indexed file.

The basic processing requirements are:

1. Read a sequential inventory record.

2. Write an indexed inventory record.

Figure 2-9   The program overview for a key-sequenced file-creation program

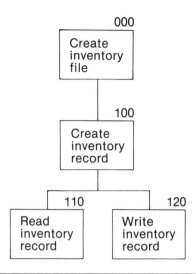

Figure 2-10   The structure chart for the file creation program

When you create a key-sequenced file, you can use a non-VSAM sequential file or an ESDS to provide the data for each KSDS record. Since the indexed records must be written in key sequence, the input records must also be in key sequence. If they aren't, you have to sort them before you can run a file-creation program. In addition, you have to use AMS to define the new KSDS before you run this type of program. I'll show you how to do that in chapter 6.

Incidentally, you can perform the same function as this program using a single AMS command. So you'll probably never code a program like this one. On the other hand, if the file creation requires you to rearrange data in a record or combine data from several records, you'll have to code a program similar to this one.

Figure 2-11 presents the program listing. There are only four things I want to point out in this program. First, the SELECT statement for the key-sequenced file shows that the file has indexed organization and will be accessed sequentially. It also specifies that the key field for the file is IR-ITEM-NO. Remember, you must specify the key field even though you access the file sequentially. The SELECT statement also specifies a FILE STATUS field called INVMSTI-ERROR-CODE that's defined in working storage.

Second, look at the record description for the key-sequenced data set in the File Section. Even though I didn't have to define each field in the record in this section, I did have to define the key field. The name of the key field has to be the same as the name of the field specified in the RECORD KEY clause of the SELECT statement.

```
 IDENTIFICATION DIVISION.
*
 PROGRAM-ID.  INV1100.
*
 ENVIRONMENT DIVISION.
*
 INPUT-OUTPUT SECTION.
*
 FILE-CONTROL.
     SELECT INVMAST ASSIGN TO SYSO20-AS-INVMAST.
     SELECT INVMSTI ASSIGN TO SYSO21-INVMSTI
                ORGANIZATION IS INDEXED
                ACCESS IS SEQUENTIAL
                RECORD KEY IS IR-ITEM-NO
                FILE STATUS IS INVMSTI-ERROR-CODE.
*
 DATA DIVISION.
*
 FILE SECTION.
*
 FD   INVMAST
      LABEL RECORDS ARE STANDARD
      RECORD CONTAINS 50 CHARACTERS.
*
 01   SEQUENTIAL-RECORD-AREA  PIC X(50).
*
 FD   INVMSTI
      LABEL RECORDS ARE STANDARD
      RECORD CONTAINS 50 CHARACTERS.
*
 01   INDEXED-RECORD-AREA.
*
     05   IR-ITEM-NO      PIC X(5).
     05   FILLER          PIC X(45).
*
 WORKING-STORAGE SECTION.
*
 01   SWITCHES.
*
     05   INVMAST-EOF-SWITCH     PIC X     VALUE 'N'.
          88  INVMAST-EOF                  VALUE 'Y'.
*
 01   FILE-STATUS-FIELD.
*
     05 INVMSTI-ERROR-CODE      PIC XX.
*
```

Figure 2-11   The file creation program (part 1 of 2)

```
01  INVENTORY-MASTER-RECORD.
*
    05  IM-DESCRIPTIVE-DATA.
        10 IM-ITEM-NUMBER       PIC X(5).
        10 IM-ITEM-DESC         PIC X(20).
        10 IM-UNIT-COST         PIC S999V99.
        10 IM-UNIT-PRICE        PIC S999V99.
    05  IM-INVENTORY-DATA.
        10  IM-REORDER-POINT    PIC S9(5).
        10  IM-ON-HAND          PIC S9(5).
        10  IM-ON-ORDER         PIC S9(5).
*
 PROCEDURE DIVISION.
*
 000-CREATE-INVENTORY-FILE.
*
    OPEN INPUT  INVMAST
         OUTPUT INVMSTI.
    PERFORM 100-CREATE-INVENTORY-RECORD
        UNTIL INVMAST-EOF.
    CLOSE INVMAST
          INVMSTI.
    DISPLAY 'INV1100  I  1   NORMAL EOJ'.
    STOP RUN.
*
 100-CREATE-INVENTORY-RECORD.
*
    PERFORM 110-READ-INVENTORY-RECORD.
    IF NOT INVMAST-EOF
        PERFORM 120-WRITE-INVENTORY-RECORD.
*
 110-READ-INVENTORY-RECORD.
*
    READ INVMAST INTO INVENTORY-MASTER-RECORD
        AT END
            MOVE 'Y' TO INVMAST-EOF-SWITCH.
*
 120-WRITE-INVENTORY-RECORD.
*
    WRITE INDEXED-RECORD-AREA FROM INVENTORY-MASTER-RECORD.
    IF INVMSTI-ERROR-CODE NOT = '00'
        DISPLAY 'INV1100  A  2   WRITE ERROR FOR INVMSTI'
        DISPLAY 'INV1100  A  2   ITEM NUMBER = ' IR-ITEM-NO
        DISPLAY 'INV1100  A  2   FILE STATUS = '
            INVMSTI-ERROR-CODE
        MOVE 'Y' TO INVMAST-EOF-SWITCH.
```

Figure 2-11   The file creation program (part 2 of 2)

Third, notice that I coded a single record description in the Working-Storage Section for both the sequential file and the KSDS. I was able to do this because the records have the same format. Then, when the program reads a record from the sequential file, the INTO clause in the READ statement places the record into this area in the Working-Storage Section. And when the program writes a record to the KSDS, the FROM clause in the WRITE statement writes the record from this same area.

Fourth, notice in module 120 that I coded an IF statement to check the FILE STATUS field, INVMSTI-ERROR-CODE, after the WRITE statement. If the error code is not zero, module 120 displays an error message and ends the program by turning on the end-of-file switch.

I didn't code an INVALID KEY clause after the WRITE statement in module 120 because the system only executes this clause when certain conditions occur. In other words, there are some I/O errors in VSAM that the INVALID KEY clause doesn't catch. That's why we recommend that you always omit the INVALID KEY clause for VSAM files. Instead, you should code an IF statement that tests the FILE STATUS field and takes the necessary action based on the value of that field. You'll see this technique used in all of the program examples in this topic. And I'll explain more about error processing in the next topic.

A sequential update program   When you update a key-sequenced data set on a sequential basis, you read transaction records one at a time in the order of the key field of the master file. Then, after the record is updated, a REWRITE statement writes the master record back into the location it was originally read from. This is sometimes referred to as an update-in-place procedure.

Figure 2-12 presents a program overview for a sequential update program. The records in the inventory master file are updated based on the data in a file of valid inventory transactions. After all transactions for an item have been processed, the record is rewritten to the file.

Figure 2-13 presents the structure chart for this program. Here, module 300 is the main control module. It controls the reading of the transaction and master files and determines what update action to take based on a comparison of the control fields in the transaction and master records.

The complete source listing for this program is shown in figure 2-14. Except for minor name changes, the SELECT and FD statements for the inventory file, INVMAST, are the same as those in the file-creation program. In the Procedure Division, however, I opened the file as I-O. This allows the REWRITE statement to replace the updated records in their original locations.

Program:	INV1200 Update inventory file (sequential)	Page: 1

Designer: Mike Murach	Date: 09-03-86

Input/output specifications

File	Description	Use
VALTRAN	Valid inventory transaction file	Input
INVMAST	Inventory master file	Update
ERRTRAN	Unmatched inventory transaction file	Output

Process specifications

This program updates an inventory master file (INVMAST) based on the data in a sequential file of valid inventory transaction records (VALTRAN). It reads the master file on a sequential basis and rewrites the updated records on the master file. The master file is indexed by item number.

If a transaction has the same item number as a master record, the transaction matches the master record. Then, the program uses the transaction data to update the master record. It does this by increasing the on hand quantity in the master record by the receipt quantity in the transaction record.

If the program can't find a matching master record for a transaction, the transaction is unmatched. Then, the program writes the transaction record on the file of error transactions (ERRTRAN).

VALTRAN is in sequence by item number. Since INVMAST is being accessed sequentially, its records are also retrieved in item-number sequence. Also, the record formats for VALTRAN and ERRTRAN are the same.

The basic processing requirements are:

1. Read a transaction record.

2. If necessary, get inventory master records until a record with a matching or greater item number is found. This step includes rewriting the last master record that was updated.

3. If the transaction is matched, update the matching master record.

4. If the transaction is unmatched, write the record on the file of error transactions.

Figure 2-12   The program overview for a program that sequentially updates an indexed file

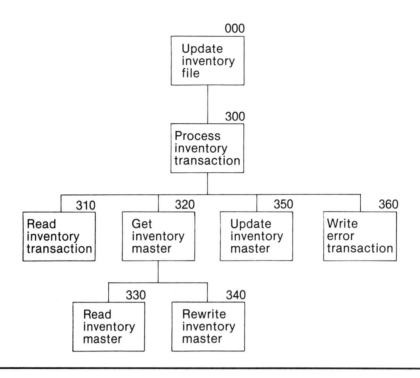

Figure 2-13   The structure chart for the sequential update program

If you study the logic in modules 300 and 320, I'm sure you'll understand it. So don't take too much time with it now. Instead, look at the modules that perform I/O functions on the VSAM key-sequenced file.

In module 330, I didn't code an AT END clause after the READ operation. Instead, I checked the FILE STATUS field, INVMAST-ERROR-CODE. If the error code is 10, I know I've reached the end of the file (see figure 2-8 for the error codes). Any other error code indicates a more serious error, so I end the program by turning on the ALL-RECORDS-PROCESSED-SWITCH.

In module 340, the error handling is the same as that in the file-creation program. Since the INVALID KEY clause doesn't catch all possible errors, I coded an IF statement to check the FILE STATUS field after the REWRITE statement. If the error code is anything other than 00, the program displays an error message and ends the program.

```
 IDENTIFICATION DIVISION.
*
 PROGRAM-ID.  INV1200.
*
 ENVIRONMENT DIVISION.
*
 INPUT-OUTPUT SECTION.
*
 FILE-CONTROL.
     SELECT VALTRAN   ASSIGN TO SYS020-AS-VALTRAN.
     SELECT INVMAST   ASSIGN TO SYS021-INVMAST
                      ORGANIZATION IS INDEXED
                      ACCESS IS SEQUENTIAL
                      RECORD KEY IS MR-ITEM-NO
                      FILE STATUS IS INVMAST-ERROR-CODE.
     SELECT ERRTRAN   ASSIGN TO SYS022-AS-ERRTRAN.
*
 DATA DIVISION.
*
 FILE SECTION.
*
 FD  VALTRAN
     LABEL RECORDS ARE STANDARD
     RECORD CONTAINS 21 CHARACTERS.
*
 01  VALID-TRANSACTION-AREA      PIC X(21).
*
 FD  INVMAST
     LABEL RECORDS ARE STANDARD
     RECORD CONTAINS 50 CHARACTERS.
*
 01  MASTER-RECORD-AREA.
*
     05  MR-ITEM-NO             PIC X(5).
     05  FILLER                 PIC X(45).
*
 FD  ERRTRAN
     LABEL RECORDS ARE STANDARD
     RECORD CONTAINS 21 CHARACTERS.
*
 01  ERROR-TRANSACTION          PIC X(21).
*
```

Figure 2-14   The sequential update program (part 1 of 4)

```
WORKING-STORAGE SECTION.
*
 01  SWITCHES.
*
     05  ALL-RECORDS-PROCESSED-SWITCH    PIC X    VALUE 'N'.
         88  ALL-RECORDS-PROCESSED                VALUE 'Y'.
     05  MASTER-UPDATED-SWITCH           PIC X    VALUE 'N'.
         88  MASTER-UPDATED                       VALUE 'Y'.
*
 01  FILE-STATUS-FIELD.
*
     05  INVMAST-ERROR-CODE      PIC XX.
*
 01  INVENTORY-TRANSACTION-RECORD.
*
     05  IT-ITEM-NO              PIC X(5).
     05  IT-VENDOR-NO            PIC X(5).
     05  IT-RECEIPT-DATE         PIC X(6).
     05  IT-RECEIPT-QUANTITY     PIC S9(5).
*
 01  INVENTORY-MASTER-RECORD.
*
     05  IM-DESCRIPTIVE-DATA.
         10  IM-ITEM-NO          PIC X(5).
         10  IM-ITEM-DESC        PIC X(20).
         10  IM-UNIT-COST        PIC S999V99.
         10  IM-UNIT-PRICE       PIC S999V99.
     05  IM-INVENTORY-DATA.
         10  IM-REORDER-POINT    PIC S9(5).
         10  IM-ON-HAND          PIC S9(5).
         10  IM-ON-ORDER         PIC S9(5).
*
 PROCEDURE DIVISION.
*
 000-UPDATE-INVENTORY-FILE.
*
     OPEN INPUT   VALTRAN
          I-O     INVMAST
          OUTPUT ERRTRAN.
     MOVE LOW-VALUE TO IM-ITEM-NO.
     PERFORM 300-PROCESS-INVENTORY-TRAN
         UNTIL ALL-RECORDS-PROCESSED.
     CLOSE VALTRAN
           INVMAST
           ERRTRAN.
     DISPLAY 'INV1200  I  1  NORMAL EOJ'.
     STOP RUN.
*
```

Figure 2-14   The sequential update program (part 2 of 4)

```
300-PROCESS-INVENTORY-TRAN.
*
    PERFORM 310-READ-INVENTORY-TRAN.
    PERFORM 320-GET-INVENTORY-MASTER
        UNTIL IM-ITEM-NO NOT < IT-ITEM-NO.
    IF          IM-ITEM-NO = HIGH-VALUE
          AND IT-ITEM-NO = HIGH-VALUE
        MOVE 'Y' TO ALL-RECORDS-PROCESSED-SWITCH
    ELSE
        IF IM-ITEM-NO = IT-ITEM-NO
            PERFORM 350-UPDATE-INVENTORY-MASTER
        ELSE
            PERFORM 360-WRITE-ERROR-TRAN.
*
 310-READ-INVENTORY-TRAN.
*
    READ VALTRAN INTO INVENTORY-TRANSACTION-RECORD
        AT END
            MOVE HIGH-VALUE TO IT-ITEM-NO.
*
 320-GET-INVENTORY-MASTER.
*
    IF MASTER-UPDATED
        PERFORM 340-REWRITE-INVENTORY-MASTER
        PERFORM 330-READ-INVENTORY-MASTER
    ELSE
        PERFORM 330-READ-INVENTORY-MASTER.
*
 330-READ-INVENTORY-MASTER.
*
    READ INVMAST INTO INVENTORY-MASTER-RECORD.
    IF INVMAST-ERROR-CODE NOT = '00'
        IF INVMAST-ERROR-CODE = '10'
            MOVE HIGH-VALUE TO IM-ITEM-NO
        ELSE
            MOVE 'Y' TO ALL-RECORDS-PROCESSED-SWITCH.
*
 340-REWRITE-INVENTORY-MASTER.
*
    REWRITE MASTER-RECORD-AREA FROM INVENTORY-MASTER-RECORD.
    IF INVMAST-ERROR-CODE NOT = '00'
        DISPLAY 'INV1200   A   2   REWRITE ERROR FOR INVMAST'
        DISPLAY 'INV1200   A   2   ITEM NUMBER = ' IM-ITEM-NO
        DISPLAY 'INV1200   A   2   FILE STATUS = '
            INVMAST-ERROR-CODE
        MOVE 'Y' TO ALL-RECORDS-PROCESSED-SWITCH.
    MOVE 'N' TO MASTER-UPDATED-SWITCH.
*
```

Figure 2-14   The sequential update program (part 3 of 4)

```
350-UPDATE-INVENTORY-MASTER.
*
    ADD IT-RECEIPT-QUANTITY TO IM-ON-HAND.
    MOVE 'Y' TO MASTER-UPDATED-SWITCH.
*
 360-WRITE-ERROR-TRAN.
*
    WRITE ERROR-TRANSACTION FROM INVENTORY-TRANSACTION-RECORD.
```

Figure 2-14   The sequential update program (part 4 of 4)

Random processing

When you process an indexed file randomly, you can access its records in
any order you like. To select a record, you must first place the key value
of the record you want into the RECORD KEY field. Then, you issue an
I/O statement to process that record.

Figure 2-15 summarizes the COBOL elements for processing key-
sequenced files randomly. Although there are no new statements here,
there are a few variations from the statements for sequential processing
that you should be aware of. After I discuss these variations, I'll present
a random update program that uses some of these COBOL elements.

The SELECT statement

The only difference in the SELECT statement for random processing is
that you must specify RANDOM access in the ACCESS MODE clause.
All the other clauses are coded the same as they are for sequential
processing.

The READ, WRITE, REWRITE, and DELETE statements

During random processing, the READ, WRITE, REWRITE, and
DELETE statements all depend on the value in the RECORD KEY field
for their operation. Before you execute a READ statement, for example,
you must place the key of the record you want into the RECORD KEY
field. Then, when you issue the READ statement, the system attempts
to read the record with that key. If there isn't a record with that key, an
INVALID KEY condition occurs. Similarly, the DELETE statement
knows which record to delete by the value in the RECORD KEY field.
And the WRITE and REWRITE statements use the RECORD KEY
values to write and rewrite records in their proper file locations. You use
the WRITE statement to add records to a file and the REWRITE statement to update records in their original locations.

SELECT statement

```
SELECT file-name
     ASSIGN TO system-name
     ORGANIZATION IS INDEXED
     ACCESS MODE IS RANDOM
     RECORD KEY IS data-name-1
     [FILE STATUS IS data-name-2]
```

Note: The RECORD KEY field must be defined in the File Section as a field within the record description. And the FILE STATUS field must be defined in working storage as a two-byte alphanumeric item.

FD statement

```
FD  file-name
     LABEL RECORDS ARE STANDARD
     [RECORD CONTAINS integer CHARACTERS]
```

Procedure Division statements

```
      (INPUT   file-name-1 ...)
OPEN  {OUTPUT  file-name-2 ...}
      (I-O     file-name-3 ...)

READ file-name RECORD
     [INTO identifier]
     [INVALID KEY imperative-statement]


WRITE record-name
     [FROM identifier]
     [INVALID KEY imperative-statement]


REWRITE record-name
     [FROM identifier]
     [INVALID KEY imperative-statement]


DELETE file-name RECORD
     [INVALID KEY imperative-statement]


CLOSE file-name ...
```

Figure 2-15   COBOL elements for random processing of key-sequenced files

Once again, I recommend that you omit the INVALID KEY clauses in I/O statements for VSAM files. Since the system executes this clause for only a limited number of error conditions, any other problem will go undetected. As a result, it's better to test the FILE STATUS field with IF statements following each I/O operation. That way, you can be sure your program performs the appropriate error-handling functions.

A random update program

Figure 2-16 presents a program overview for a program that updates an indexed file of inventory records based on the data in a sequential file of valid inventory transactions. This program is just like the sequential update program I presented earlier in this topic, except it processes the records on a random basis.

As you can see in the program overview, I've assumed the transaction file is in no particular sequence, so the program reads a transaction record, reads the master record with the same key as the transaction record, updates the master record, and then rewrites it. If the transaction file were in sequence by record key, however, this would be inefficient. In that case, the program should check to make sure it has processed all the transactions for the master record before it rewrites the updated record to the file.

Figure 2-17 presents the structure chart for this program. It has modules to read an inventory transaction record, to read the matching master record, to update the data in the master record, to rewrite the master record, and to write an error transaction. Module 300 controls all these operations.

Figure 2-18 presents the source code for this program. It should be easy for you to understand. In the Environment Division, the only difference from the sequential update program is that the SELECT statement for the inventory master file specifies RANDOM access. The logic in the Procedure Division is a little different, too. If you take a minute to study module 300, though, I'm sure you'll see how it works.

Notice the error handling in module 320, where the program reads an inventory master record. After the program moves the item number of the transaction record to the key field of the master record, MR-ITEM-NO, it issues a READ statement. Then, after the READ statement, the program tests the FILE STATUS field, INVMAST-ERROR-CODE. If it's zero, the program turns on the MASTER-FOUND-SWITCH. If it's not zero, an error has occurred, so the program turns the switch off.

Program:	INV1300 Update inventory file (random)	**Page:** 1
Designer: Mike Murach		**Date:** 09-03-86

Input/output specifications

File	Description	Use
VALTRAN	Valid inventory transaction file	Input
INVMAST	Inventory master file	Update
ERRTRAN	Unmatched inventory transaction file	Output

Process specifications

This program updates an inventory master file (INVMAST) based on the data in a sequential file of valid inventory transaction records (VALTRAN). The inventory master file is indexed by item number and updated randomly.

If the program finds a master record with the same item number as a transaction, it uses the transaction data to update the master record. It does this by increasing the on hand quantity in the master record by the receipt quantity in the transaction record.

If the program can't find a master record for a transaction, it writes the transaction record on the file of error transactions (ERRTRAN). The record format for ERRTRAN is the same as for VALTRAN.

The basic processing requirements are:

1. Read a transaction record.

2. Read the master record with the same item number as in the transaction record.

3. If the master record is found, update and rewrite the matching master record.

4. If the transaction is not found, write the transaction record on the file of error transactions.

Figure 2-16   The program overview for a program that randomly updates an indexed file

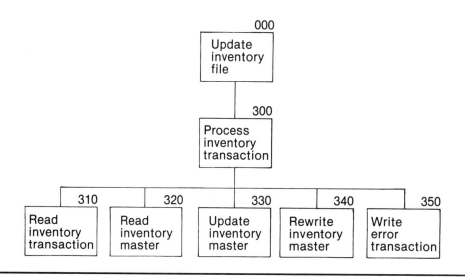

Figure 2-17   The structure chart for the random update program

Dynamic processing

Some programs require that you use a mixture of sequential and random access. This can be referred to as *dynamic processing*, or *dynamic access* of key-sequenced files.

Before I show you how to use dynamic processing, I want you to realize that you may never have the need for it in COBOL. After all, most programs require nothing more than simple sequential or random processing. Still, some batch programs require you to use dynamic access so you can switch between sequential and random access. And I know of some shops that use dynamic access in *all* programs, whether it's needed or not. So you need to understand how it works.

The COBOL elements for dynamic processing

With dynamic access, you can use the COBOL elements presented in the sequential processing summary in figure 2-6 as well as the COBOL elements presented in the random processing summary in figure 2-15. The only statements that have special formats for dynamic processing are the SELECT statement and the sequential READ statement, as shown in figure 2-19.

```
IDENTIFICATION DIVISION.
*
 PROGRAM-ID.  INV1300.
*
 ENVIRONMENT DIVISION.
*
 INPUT-OUTPUT SECTION.
*
 FILE-CONTROL.
     SELECT VALTRAN  ASSIGN TO SYS020-AS-VALTRAN.
     SELECT INVMAST  ASSIGN TO SYS021-INVMAST
                     ORGANIZATION IS INDEXED
                     ACCESS IS RANDOM
                     RECORD KEY IS MR-ITEM-NO
                     FILE STATUS IS INVMAST-ERROR-CODE.
     SELECT ERRTRAN  ASSIGN TO SYS022-AS-ERRTRAN.
*
 DATA DIVISION.
*
 FILE SECTION.
*
 FD  VALTRAN
     LABEL RECORDS ARE STANDARD
     RECORD CONTAINS 21 CHARACTERS.
*
 01  VALID-TRANSACTION-AREA        PIC X(21).
*
 FD  INVMAST
     LABEL RECORDS ARE STANDARD
     RECORD CONTAINS 50 CHARACTERS.
*
 01  MASTER-RECORD-AREA.
*
     05  MR-ITEM-NO                PIC X(5).
     05  FILLER                    PIC X(45).
*
 FD  ERRTRAN
     LABEL RECORDS ARE STANDARD
     RECORD CONTAINS 21 CHARACTERS.
*
 01  ERROR-TRANSACTION             PIC X(21).
*
```

Figure 2-18   The random update program (part 1 of 3)

```
WORKING-STORAGE SECTION.
*
01  SWITCHES.
*
    05  VALTRAN-EOF-SWITCH          PIC X    VALUE 'N'.
        88  VALTRAN-EOF                      VALUE 'Y'.
    05  MASTER-FOUND-SWITCH        PIC X.
        88  MASTER-FOUND                     VALUE 'Y'.
*
01  FILE-STATUS-FIELD.
*
    05  INVMAST-ERROR-CODE         PIC XX.
*
01  INVENTORY-TRANSACTION-RECORD.
*
    05  IT-ITEM-NO                 PIC X(5).
    05  IT-VENDOR-NO               PIC X(5).
    05  IT-RECEIPT-DATE            PIC X(6).
    05  IT-RECEIPT-QUANTITY        PIC S9(5).
*
01  INVENTORY-MASTER-RECORD.
*
    05  IM-DESCRIPTIVE-DATA.
        10  IM-ITEM-NO             PIC X(5).
        10  IM-ITEM-DESC           PIC X(20).
        10  IM-UNIT-COST           PIC S999V99.
        10  IM-UNIT-PRICE          PIC S999V99.
    05  IM-INVENTORY-DATA.
        10  IM-REORDER-POINT       PIC S9(5).
        10  IM-ON-HAND             PIC S9(5).
        10  IM-ON-ORDER            PIC S9(5).
*
 PROCEDURE DIVISION.
*
 000-UPDATE-INVENTORY-FILE.
*
    OPEN INPUT   VALTRAN
         I-O     INVMAST
         OUTPUT ERRTRAN.
    PERFORM 300-PROCESS-INVENTORY-TRAN
        UNTIL VALTRAN-EOF.
    CLOSE VALTRAN
          INVMAST
          ERRTRAN.
    DISPLAY 'INV1300  I  1  NORMAL EOJ'.
    STOP RUN.
*
```

Figure 2-18   The random update program (part 2 of 3)

```
 300-PROCESS-INVENTORY-TRAN.
*
     PERFORM 310-READ-INVENTORY-TRAN.
     IF NOT VALTRAN-EOF
         PERFORM 320-READ-INVENTORY-MASTER
         IF MASTER-FOUND
             PERFORM 330-UPDATE-INVENTORY-MASTER
             PERFORM 340-REWRITE-INVENTORY-MASTER
         ELSE
             PERFORM 350-WRITE-ERROR-TRAN.
*
 310-READ-INVENTORY-TRAN.
*
     READ VALTRAN INTO INVENTORY-TRANSACTION-RECORD
         AT END
             MOVE 'Y' TO VALTRAN-EOF-SWITCH.
*
 320-READ-INVENTORY-MASTER.
*
     MOVE IT-ITEM-NO TO MR-ITEM-NO.
     READ INVMAST INTO INVENTORY-MASTER-RECORD.
     IF INVMAST-ERROR-CODE = '00'
         MOVE 'Y' TO MASTER-FOUND-SWITCH
     ELSE
         MOVE 'N' TO MASTER-FOUND-SWITCH.
*
 330-UPDATE-INVENTORY-MASTER.
*
     ADD IT-RECEIPT-QUANTITY TO IM-ON-HAND.
*
 340-REWRITE-INVENTORY-MASTER.
*
     REWRITE MASTER-RECORD-AREA FROM INVENTORY-MASTER-RECORD.
     IF INVMAST-ERROR-CODE NOT = '00'
         DISPLAY 'INV1300  A 2   REWRITE ERROR FOR INVMAST'
         DISPLAY 'INV1300  A 2   ITEM NUMBER = ' IM-ITEM-NO
         DISPLAY 'INV1300  A 2   FILE STATUS = '
             INVMAST-ERROR-CODE
         MOVE 'Y' TO VALTRAN-EOF-SWITCH.
*
 350-WRITE-ERROR-TRAN.
*
     WRITE ERROR-TRANSACTION FROM INVENTORY-TRANSACTION-RECORD.
```

Figure 2-18   The random update program (part 3 of 3)

SELECT statement

```
SELECT file-name
    ASSIGN TO system-name
    ORGANIZATION IS INDEXED
    ACCESS MODE IS DYNAMIC
    RECORD KEY IS data-name-1
    [FILE STATUS IS data-name-2]
```

Note: The RECORD KEY field must be defined in the File Section as a field within the record description.
And the FILE STATUS field must be defined in working storage as a two-byte alphanumeric item.

Sequential READ statement

```
READ file-name NEXT RECORD
    [INTO identifier]
    [AT END imperative-statement]
```

Random READ statement

```
READ file-name RECORD
    [INTO identifier]
    [INVALID KEY imperative-statement]
```

Figure 2-19   COBOL elements for dynamic processing of key-sequenced files

To use dynamic access, you code ACCESS IS DYNAMIC in the
SELECT statement for your files. All the other clauses are coded the
same as they are for sequential and random access.

When you specify dynamic access, you can read records sequentially
or randomly, depending on how you code the READ statement. If you
specify NEXT on the READ statement, your program will retrieve
records sequentially. If you omit NEXT, your program will retrieve
records randomly based on the value in the RECORD KEY field.

The WRITE, REWRITE and DELETE statements work the same for
dynamic access as they do for random access. In other words, they
depend on the value in the RECORD KEY field. The START statement,
on the other hand, works as it does for sequential access; it establishes
the starting position for sequential retrieval.

The key to using dynamic access is knowing how to switch from
sequential to random access. The position for sequential retrieval is
changed only by a START or a random READ statement. As a result,
you can issue a random READ statement to retrieve a specific record,

then issue a sequential READ statement (using the NEXT option) to retrieve each record sequentially from that point. If you issue a WRITE, REWRITE, or DELETE statement, file positioning doesn't change.

A report preparation program that uses dynamic access

Figure 2-20 presents the program specifications for a report preparation program that processes an indexed file of inventory location records. For each inventory transaction, which represents a receipt to inventory, the program is supposed to list all of the inventory locations where some stock for that item number is stored. As you can deduce from the print chart, one line is printed for each inventory location record that is read for an item.

For each inventory item, there may be from zero to 99 location records in the inventory location file. The key for the location file consists of the item number followed by a two-digit sequence number. The first location record for each item number has a sequence number of 01; the second record has a sequence number of 02; and so on. Because of this, the program that prepares the report could read the location records using random access. To illustrate dynamic access, though, the program will read the first location record for each inventory item randomly. Then, it will read the other records for the item sequentially.

Figure 2-21 presents the structure chart for this program. To support dynamic access, module 320 prepares only the first location line for each transaction record, and module 330 reads the first location record on a random basis. Then, module 340 prepares the location lines for the other location records for each transaction record, and module 350 reads the remaining location records on a sequential basis.

Figure 2-22 presents the COBOL code for this program. Since it merely combines the sequential and random access code you've already learned into a single program, you should be able to understand it without much trouble.

Notice what happens in module 330. First, the program builds the key for the transaction's first location record by moving the item number from the transaction record to the location key's item-number field and 01 to the location key's sequence-number field. Then, the program reads the first location record. Next, it checks the return code, INVLOC-ERROR-CODE, to make sure there weren't any errors during the execution of the READ statement. If INVLOC-ERROR-CODE is 00, the READ was successful, and there's at least one location record for the item. So the program turns the LOCATION-FOUND-SWITCH on. Otherwise, it turns the switch off.

After module 330 reads the first location record for a transaction on a random basis, module 350 reads the subsequent location records on a

Program:	INV1400 Prepare location listing	Page: 1
Designer:	Mike Murach	Date: 09-03-86

Input/output specifications

File	Description	Use
VALTRAN	Valid inventory transaction file	Input
INVLOC	Inventory location file	Update
LOCLIST	Print file: Inventory location listing	Output

Process specifications

This program reads a sequential file of valid transaction records (VALTRAN) that represent receipts to inventory. These records are in a random sequence. As the program reads this file, it prints a listing of the possible inventory locations where each inventory item can be stored. It gets these locations from a file of location records (INVLOC).

The inventory location file is an indexed file. The key for each record is made up of an item number and a sequence number. The sequence number ranges from 01 through as many different location records as there are for an item number. If, for example, item number 23354 has five location records that apply to it, the location record keys are 2335401, 2335402, 2335403, 2335404, and 2335405.

The basic processing requirements are:

1. Read a transaction record.

2. Read all the location records for the item number represented by the transaction. For each location record, print a line on the location listing. If there are no location records for a transaction, print a line on the location listing that indicates that no location records have been found.

Figure 2-20   The program specifications for a report preparation program that dynamically retrieves the records in a KSDS (part 1 of 2)

The record layout for the inventory transaction file

```
01    INVENTORY-TRANSACTION-RECORD.
*
      05   IT-ITEM-NUMBER                PIC X(5).
      05   IT-VENDOR-NUMBER             PIC X(5).
      05   IT-RECEIPT-DATE              PIC X(6).
      05   IT-RECEIPT-QUANTITY          PIC S9(5).
```

The record layout for the inventory location file

```
01    INVENTORY-LOCATION-RECORD.
*
      05   IL-RECORD-KEY.
           10   IL-ITEM-NO              PIC X(5).
           10   IL-SEQUENCE-NO          PIC XX.
      05   IL-LOCATION-DATA.
           10   IL-WAREHOUSE-NO         PIC X(2).
           10   IL-LOCATION-NO          PIC X(4).
           10   IL-BIN-NO               PIC X(2).
           10   IL-CAPACITY             PIC S9(5).
           10   IL-QUANTITY-STORED      PIC S9(5).
           10   IL-QUANTITY-AVAILABLE   PIC S9(5).
```

The print chart for the inventory location listing

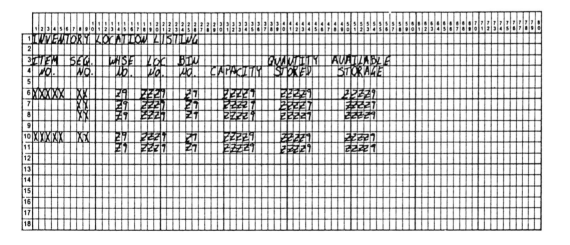

Figure 2-20   The program specifications for a report preparation program that dynamically retrieves the records in a KSDS (part 2 of 2)

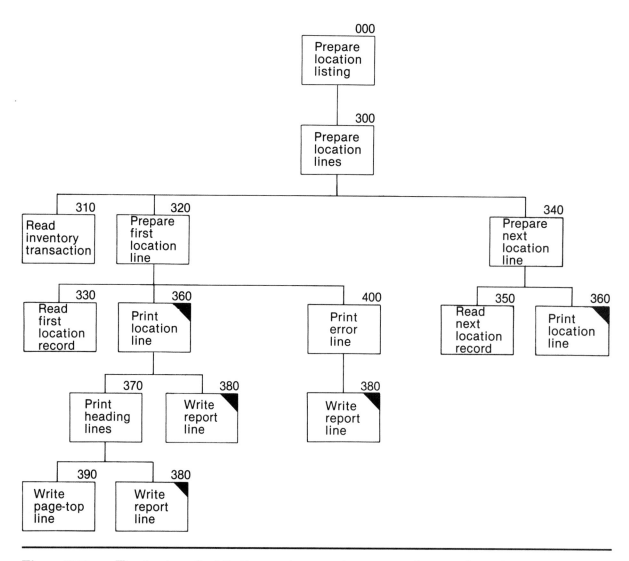

Figure 2-21   The structure chart for the report preparation program that uses dynamic access

sequential basis. Note that I coded the word NEXT in the READ statement in module 350 to indicate sequential access. After the program reads the next location record, I compare the item number in the transaction record with the item number in the location record. If they're equal, LOCATION-FOUND-SWITCH remains on. If they're not equal, the program turns the switch off so the program can continue with the next transaction record.

```
IDENTIFICATION DIVISION.
*
PROGRAM-ID.  INV1400.
*
ENVIRONMENT DIVISION.
*
INPUT-OUTPUT SECTION.
*
FILE-CONTROL.
    SELECT VALTRAN   ASSIGN TO SYS020-AS-VALTRAN.
    SELECT INVLOC    ASSIGN TO SYS021-INVLOC
                     ORGANIZATION IS INDEXED
                     ACCESS IS DYNAMIC
                     RECORD KEY IS LR-RECORD-KEY
                     FILE STATUS IS INVLOC-ERROR-CODE.
    SELECT LOCLIST   ASSIGN TO SYS006-UR-1403-S.
*
DATA DIVISION.
*
FILE SECTION.
*
FD  VALTRAN
    LABEL RECORDS ARE STANDARD
    RECORD CONTAINS 21 CHARACTERS.
*
01  VALID-TRANSACTION-AREA      PIC X(21).
*
FD  INVLOC
    LABEL RECORDS ARE STANDARD
    RECORD CONTAINS 30 CHARACTERS.
*
01  LOCATION-RECORD-AREA.
*
    05  LR-RECORD-KEY.
        10  LR-ITEM-NO          PIC X(5).
        10  LR-SEQUENCE-NO      PIC XX.
    05  FILLER                  PIC X(23).
*
FD  LOCLIST
    LABEL RECORDS ARE OMITTED
    RECORD CONTAINS 132 CHARACTERS.
*
01  PRINT-AREA                  PIC X(132).
*
```

Figure 2-22   The report preparation program that uses dynamic access (part 1 of 6)

```
WORKING-STORAGE SECTION.
*
 01   SWITCHES.
*
      05   VALTRAN-EOF-SWITCH      PIC X      VALUE 'N'.
           88   VALTRAN-EOF                   VALUE 'Y'.
      05   LOCATION-FOUND-SWITCH   PIC X.
           88   LOCATION-FOUND                VALUE 'Y'.
*
 01   FILE-STATUS-FIELD.
*
      05   INVLOC-ERROR-CODE       PIC XX.
*
 01   PRINT-FIELDS               COMP-3.
*
      05   SPACE-CONTROL           PIC S9.
      05   LINES-ON-PAGE           PIC S999  VALUE +55.
      05   LINE-COUNT              PIC S999  VALUE +99.
*
 01   INVENTORY-TRANSACTION.
*
      05   IT-ITEM-NO              PIC X(5).
      05   IT-VENDOR-NO            PIC X(5).
      05   IT-RECEIPT-DATE         PIC X(6).
      05   IT-RECEIPT-QUANTITY     PIC S9(5).
*
 01   INVENTORY-LOCATION-RECORD.
*
      05   IL-RECORD-KEY.
           10   IL-ITEM-NO              PIC X(5).
           10   IL-SEQUENCE-NO          PIC XX.
      05   IL-LOCATION-DATA.
           10   IL-WAREHOUSE-NO         PIC X(2).
           10   IL-LOCATION-NO          PIC X(4).
           10   IL-BIN-NO               PIC X(2).
           10   IL-CAPACITY             PIC S9(5).
           10   IL-QUANTITY-STORED      PIC S9(5).
           10   IL-QUANTITY-AVAILABLE   PIC S9(5).
*
 01   HEADING-LINE-1.
*
      05   FILLER  PIC X(30)   VALUE 'INVENTORY LOCATION LISTING'.
      05   FILLER  PIC X(102)  VALUE SPACE.
*
```

Figure 2-22   The report preparation program that uses dynamic access (part 2 of 6)

```
 01   HEADING-LINE-2.
*
     05   FILLER  PIC X(20)   VALUE 'ITEM  SEQ.   WHSE   LO'.
     05   FILLER  PIC X(20)   VALUE 'C  BIN              QUA'.
     05   FILLER  PIC X(20)   VALUE 'NTITY  AVAILABLE      '.
     05   FILLER  PIC X(72)   VALUE SPACE.
*
 01   HEADING-LINE-3.
*
     05   FILLER  PIC X(20)   VALUE ' NO.    NO.    NO.    NO'.
     05   FILLER  PIC X(20)   VALUE '. NO.  CAPACITY   ST'.
     05   FILLER  PIC X(20)   VALUE 'ORED      STORAGE       '.
     05   FILLER  PIC X(72)   VALUE SPACE.
*
 01   LOCATION-LINE.
*
     05   LL-ITEM-NO              PIC X(5).
     05   FILLER                  PIC X(2)    VALUE SPACE.
     05   LL-SEQUENCE-NO          PIC X(2).
     05   FILLER                  PIC X(4)    VALUE SPACE.
     05   LL-WAREHOUSE-NO         PIC Z9.
     05   FILLER                  PIC X(2)    VALUE SPACE.
     05   LL-LOCATION-NO          PIC ZZZ9.
     05   FILLER                  PIC X(3)    VALUE SPACE.
     05   LL-BIN-NO               PIC Z9.
     05   FILLER                  PIC X(4)    VALUE SPACE.
     05   LL-CAPACITY             PIC ZZZZ9.
     05   FILLER                  PIC X(4)    VALUE SPACE.
     05   LL-QUANTITY-STORED      PIC ZZZZ9.
     05   FILLER                  PIC X(5)    VALUE SPACE.
     05   LL-QUANTITY-AVAILABLE   PIC ZZZZ9.
     05   FILLER                  PIC X(78)   VALUE SPACE.
*
 01   LOCATION-ERROR-LINE.
*
     05   LEL-ITEM-NO             PIC X(5).
     05   FILLER                  PIC XX      VALUE SPACE.
     05   FILLER                  PIC X(24)
                                  VALUE 'NO LOCATION RECORD FOUND'.
     05   FILLER                  PIC X(101) VALUE SPACE.
*
```

Figure 2-22   The report preparation program that uses dynamic access (part 3 of 6)

```
 PROCEDURE DIVISION.
*
 000-PREPARE-LOCATION-LISTING.
*
     OPEN INPUT  VALTRAN
                 INVLOC
          OUTPUT LOCLIST.
     PERFORM 300-PREPARE-LOCATION-LINES
         UNTIL VALTRAN-EOF.
     CLOSE VALTRAN
           INVLOC
           LOCLIST.
     DISPLAY 'INV1400  I  1  NORMAL EOJ'.
     STOP RUN.
*
 300-PREPARE-LOCATION-LINES.
*
     PERFORM 310-READ-INVENTORY-TRAN.
     IF NOT VALTRAN-EOF
         PERFORM 320-PREPARE-FIRST-LOC-LINE
         IF LOCATION-FOUND
             PERFORM 340-PREPARE-NEXT-LOCATION-LINE
                 UNTIL NOT LOCATION-FOUND.
*
 310-READ-INVENTORY-TRAN.
*
     READ VALTRAN INTO INVENTORY-TRANSACTION
         AT END
             MOVE 'Y' TO VALTRAN-EOF-SWITCH.
*
 320-PREPARE-FIRST-LOC-LINE.
*
     PERFORM 330-READ-FIRST-LOCATION-RECORD.
     MOVE 2 TO SPACE-CONTROL.
     IF LOCATION-FOUND
         PERFORM 360-PRINT-LOCATION-LINE
     ELSE
         PERFORM 400-PRINT-ERROR-LINE.
*
 330-READ-FIRST-LOCATION-RECORD.
*
     MOVE IT-ITEM-NO TO LR-ITEM-NO.
     MOVE '01'       TO LR-SEQUENCE-NO.
     READ INVLOC INTO INVENTORY-LOCATION-RECORD.
     IF INVLOC-ERROR-CODE = '00'
         MOVE 'Y' TO LOCATION-FOUND-SWITCH
     ELSE
         MOVE 'N' TO LOCATION-FOUND-SWITCH.
*
```

Figure 2-22   The report preparation program that uses dynamic access (part 4 of 6)

```
340-PREPARE-NEXT-LOCATION-LINE.
*
    PERFORM 350-READ-NEXT-LOCATION-RECORD.
    IF LOCATION-FOUND
        PERFORM 360-PRINT-LOCATION-LINE.
*
350-READ-NEXT-LOCATION-RECORD.
*
    READ INVLOC NEXT RECORD INTO INVENTORY-LOCATION-RECORD.
    IF INVLOC-ERROR-CODE NOT = '00'
        MOVE 'N' TO LOCATION-FOUND-SWITCH
        IF INVLOC-ERROR-CODE NOT = '10'
            MOVE 'Y' TO VALTRAN-EOF-SWITCH.
    IF IT-ITEM-NO NOT = IL-ITEM-NO
        MOVE 'N' TO LOCATION-FOUND-SWITCH.
*
360-PRINT-LOCATION-LINE.
*
    IF LINE-COUNT > LINES-ON-PAGE
        PERFORM 370-PRINT-HEADING-LINES.
    IF LR-SEQUENCE-NO = '01'
        MOVE IT-ITEM-NO          TO LL-ITEM-NO
    ELSE
        MOVE SPACE               TO LL-ITEM-NO.
    MOVE IL-SEQUENCE-NO          TO LL-SEQUENCE-NO.
    MOVE IL-WAREHOUSE-NO         TO LL-WAREHOUSE-NO.
    MOVE IL-LOCATION-NO          TO LL-LOCATION-NO.
    MOVE IL-BIN-NO               TO LL-BIN-NO.
    MOVE IL-CAPACITY             TO LL-CAPACITY.
    MOVE IL-QUANTITY-STORED      TO LL-QUANTITY-STORED.
    MOVE IL-QUANTITY-AVAILABLE TO LL-QUANTITY-AVAILABLE.
    MOVE LOCATION-LINE           TO PRINT-AREA.
    PERFORM 380-WRITE-REPORT-LINE.
    MOVE 1 TO SPACE-CONTROL.
*
370-PRINT-HEADING-LINES.
*
    PERFORM 390-WRITE-PAGE-TOP-LINE.
    MOVE HEADING-LINE-2 TO PRINT-AREA.
    MOVE 2 TO SPACE-CONTROL.
    PERFORM 380-WRITE-REPORT-LINE.
    MOVE HEADING-LINE-3 TO PRINT-AREA.
    MOVE 1 TO SPACE-CONTROL.
    PERFORM 380-WRITE-REPORT-LINE.
    MOVE 2 TO SPACE-CONTROL.
*
```

Figure 2-22   The report preparation program that uses dynamic access (part 5 of 6)

```
 380-WRITE-REPORT-LINE.
*
    WRITE PRINT-AREA
        AFTER ADVANCING SPACE-CONTROL LINES.
    ADD SPACE-CONTROL TO LINE-COUNT.
*
 390-WRITE-PAGE-TOP-LINE.
*
    WRITE PRINT-AREA FROM HEADING-LINE-1
        AFTER ADVANCING PAGE.
    MOVE 1 TO LINE-COUNT.
*
 400-PRINT-ERROR-LINE.
*
    MOVE IT-ITEM-NO TO LEL-ITEM-NO.
    MOVE LOCATION-ERROR-LINE TO PRINT-AREA.
    PERFORM 380-WRITE-REPORT-LINE.
```

Figure 2-22   The report preparation program that uses dynamic access (part 6 of 6)

Discussion

At this point, you should be able to write COBOL programs that process key-sequenced data sets. In particular, you should understand the coding requirements for sequential, random, and dynamic access of key-sequenced data sets. Before you start writing production programs, though, you need to know more about error processing, which I'll explain in the next topic.

Terminology

file name	dynamic processing
system name	dynamic access
return code	

Objective

Given specifications for a program that processes VSAM key-sequenced files, develop a COBOL program that satisfies the specifications.

Topic 3 VSAM error processing

Because of the way VSAM handles error conditions, many I/O errors
that cause COBOL programs to *abend* (*abnormally terminate*) when you
use non-VSAM access methods don't cause an abend when you use
VSAM. Instead, the FILE STATUS code is set to indicate the nature of
the problem, and control returns to the COBOL program. Depending on
the problem, an error message may or may not be printed by VSAM in
the JCL listing for the job. But whether or not one is, it's easy for
serious errors to go undetected.

Suppose, for example, that an update program for a key-sequenced
master file doesn't do a thorough job of checking for VSAM errors. When
the file was originally defined, it was given enough space for 8000
records, more than enough space for the 2000 records the file started
with. Now, however, the file has grown to 7800 records, and the program
is processing 400 addition records. When the program tries to write
record 8001 to the master file, VSAM prints a warning message in the
JCL listing and returns a FILE STATUS code of 24 to the COBOL
program indicating that there's no room for new records. But since the
program doesn't test for this error condition, it assumes that the write
operation was successful so it continues with the next transaction. By
the time the program ends, VSAM has written 200 warning messages in
the JCL listing, and the last 200 transactions haven't been added to the
file.

Although the operator should notice the 200 warning messages,
operators aren't always trained to do so. Often, the operator may only
notice that the program ended normally and think everything ran all
right so the errors go undetected. This can go on for several days. I
know of one installation that completely lost a master file and didn't
discover it for five days.

The only way to avoid problems like this is to test the FILE
STATUS code after every I/O statement for a VSAM file to make sure
that no error occurred. That's why I recommended in the last topic that
you avoid using the INVALID KEY clause in your I/O statements for
VSAM files. Instead, you should use IF statements that test the FILE
STATUS codes. Then, you can check for expected errors like no-record-
found conditions as well as unexpected errors that can cause serious
problems.

Although the programs in the last topic illustrated some basic error-
handling routines for VSAM files, the techniques they used were simplified for illustrative purposes. That's why this topic will expand on those

techniques. First, I'll present all of the FILE STATUS codes so you'll know what codes to check for in your programs. Next, I'll give you a better idea of when your programs should test for VSAM errors, and I'll show you when and how to terminate your program with an abend. Then, I'll give you some ideas about how error-handling techniques may vary from one COBOL shop to the next. I'll finish by showing you the random update program from the last topic with improved error handling code.

FILE STATUS codes

Figure 2-23 lists all of the possible FILE STATUS codes, the meanings of the codes for each I/O statement, and a recommendation for handling each error. As you can see, the codes from 00 to 23 represent common errors your programs should anticipate. In the last topic, I presented all of these codes except for the 02 code, which I'll present in the next topic.

All the codes that are 24 or higher represent serious error conditions that a COBOL program can't correct. For example, code 24 means that a file has run out of space. As a result, the recommended action for these codes is program termination.

Codes 30 and 90 represent system errors that don't often occur, so you'll seldom see these codes. Code 30 usually indicates a hardware problem such as a parity or transmission error. Code 90 indicates some type of VSAM logic error. The cause might be a bug in the COBOL compiler or in the VSAM system itself. Or, this code could occur if some VSAM system data was destroyed inadvertently.

Code 92 means an I/O statement tried to do something that isn't allowed. Common causes of this code are trying to read or write a record to a file that you haven't opened, trying to rewrite or delete a record before you've successfully read it, or trying to read a record sequentially after you've reached the end of the file. In any event, a logic problem in your COBOL program caused the error, so you should terminate the program and fix it.

Code 93 may mean one of two things. First, it may mean you didn't allocate enough virtual storage for VSAM to perform an I/O operation. If that's the case, simply allocate more storage and rerun the job. Second, code 93 may mean there's a *file contention* problem. This can happen when two programs try to access a file that doesn't allow multiple users. Sometimes, you can solve this problem by rescheduling the programs so they aren't run at the same time. But most of the time, you have to set the file's SHAREOPTIONS parameter to allow multiple users. You'll learn how to do this in chapter 6.

Some of the FILE STATUS codes (91, 95, 96, and 97) are only caused by OPEN errors. Code 91 means your COBOL program didn't

FILE STATUS code	OPEN	CLOSE	READ	WRITE	REWRITE	DELETE	START	Recommended program action
00	File successfully opened	File successfully closed	Record successfully read	Record successfully written	Record successfully rewritten	Record successfully deleted	Successful completion	Continue processing
02			Valid duplicate alternate key follows	Valid duplicate alternate key created	Valid duplicate alternate key created			Continue processing
10			End of file reached					Normal AT END processing
21				Record out of sequence (sequential access only)				Print error message and continue
22				Duplicate key				Print error message and continue
23			Record not found			Record not found	Specified key not found	Print error message and continue
24				No more space allocated to file				Terminate job
30	Uncorrectable I/O error	Uncorrectable I/O error	Uncorrectable I/O error	Uncorrectable I/O error	Uncorrectable I/O error	Uncorrectable I/O error	Uncorrectable I/O error	Terminate job
90	Unusable file; possibly an empty file opened as INPUT or I-O	VSAM logic error	VSAM logic error	VSAM logic error	VSAM logic error	VSAM logic error	VSAM logic error	Terminate job

Figure 2-23   File status codes (part 1 of 2)

FILE STATUS code	OPEN	CLOSE	READ	WRITE	REWRITE	DELETE	START	Recommended program action
91	Password failure							Terminate job
92	File already opened	File not open	File not open or end of file already reached	File not open; incorrect key for EXTEND file	File not open; no previous READ	File not open; no previous READ (sequential access)	Invalid request; probably file not open	Terminate job
93	Not enough virtual storage for VSAM task, or file contention problem	Not enough virtual storage for VSAM task, or file contention problem	Not enough virtual storage for VSAM task, or file contention problem	Not enough virtual storage for VSAM task, or file contention problem	Not enough virtual storage for VSAM task, or file contention problem	Not enough virtual storage for VSAM task, or file contention problem	Not enough virtual storage for VSAM task, or file contention problem	Terminate job
95	Conflicting file attributes							Terminate job
96	No DD or DLBL statement							Terminate job
97	File not closed by previous job							Terminate job

Figure 2-23   File status codes (part 2 of 2)

supply a proper password, so it can't access the file. If your installation uses password protection for its files, you may see this error occasionally. Code 95 means the file has conflicting attributes. For example, a COBOL program may specify that the file's record key is in positions 2-9, but you defined it in AMS with its key in positions 4-11. Code 96 means you didn't code a DD or DLBL statement for the file in your JCL.

Code 97 means the file wasn't properly closed by the last program that processed it. Since VSAM automatically issues a CLOSE before it opens a file, it's possible to continue processing after a program gets this code, but it isn't advisable. If a previous program aborted while it was processing the file, you should wait until you find out what caused it to abort before you process the file again.

When to check for VSAM errors

I've already said that you should check for errors after READ, WRITE, REWRITE, DELETE, and START statements. But you should also check for errors after OPEN and CLOSE statements.

If an error occurs on an OPEN statement, the first READ or WRITE statement for the file will fail, so you won't lose any data if you don't catch an open error. But even so, I recommend that you test the FILE STATUS code after the OPEN statement. It's only a few lines of code, but it can save you debugging time if an open error does occur.

I also recommend that you check for errors after you execute the CLOSE statement. If a close error occurs and you haven't tested for it, it won't be discovered until the next time the file is opened. That may be a few hours or a few days later. By that time, it may be difficult to find the program that caused the problem.

Is it necessary to perform detailed error checking in all COBOL programs that access VSAM files? Probably not. For simple report preparation programs and other programs that don't change the data in a VSAM file, you can get away with a limited amount of error checking. But for any program that changes the data in a VSAM file, error checking is a must.

How to terminate a program with an abend

In the last topic, I presented error checking routines that terminated the sample programs by getting back to the STOP RUN statement in the first module of the program. They did this by turning on the end-of-file or all-records-processed condition when an unrecoverable error was detected. The error checking routines also displayed appropriate error messages.

Although this method of error handling is better than none at all, it still has two serious drawbacks. First, if the system operators ignore error messages printed by the system, will they notice the error messages printed by the COBOL program? Second, because the programs were terminated by the STOP RUN statements, they terminated normally as far as the operating system is concerned. Then, if the program is part of a procedure involving several job steps, the steps following the program will still be run, even though the program didn't run as intended.

The solution to both of these problems is to provide a means for your COBOL program to abnormally terminate, or abend, when an error occurs. Since operators are trained to look for jobs that abend, they won't overlook the problem program. Also, when a job step abends, the system does not execute the steps that follow it in the job.

Although COBOL doesn't provide a direct means for abnormal program terminations, it's easy to call an assembler language subprogram for this purpose. Figure 2-24 illustrates two MVS and two VSE assembler language subprograms that will do the job. However, your shop probably has subprograms of its own that you are expected to use.

The first MVS subprogram in figure 2-24, called ABEND100, causes an abend and sets the user return code to 100. The second MVS subprogram, ABEND200, causes an abend, prints a storage dump, and sets the user return code to 200. When you use the ABEND200 subprogram, you must be sure you've defined a SYSUDUMP data set in the JCL for the program.

The first VSE subprogram in figure 2-24, called CANCEL, causes an abend without a storage dump. When you use it, though, you must make sure that you don't specify the DUMP option on the OPTION statement in the JCL for your program. Otherwise, you'll get a dump of all the main storage of your system. The second VSE subprogram, called DUMP, causes an abend with a storage dump.

Shop standards for VSAM error processing

Although the error processing techniques I've just presented are used in many COBOL shops, they are not standard throughout the industry. For instance, some shops require detailed reporting routines that indicate the specific cause of the error. Other shops require routines that pass a code back to the JCL in the special register called RETURN-CODE. Then, subsequent JCL statements test the return code to determine if the job should continue.

My point is that you should find out what your shop standards are for VSAM error handling. Although this topic presents the general tech-

MVS Subprograms

Abend without dump

```
ABEND100   START  0
           SAVE   (14,12)
           ABEND  100
           END
```

Abend with dump

```
ABEND200   START  0
           SAVE   (14,12)
           ABEND  200,DUMP
           END
```

DOS/VSE Subprograms

Abend without dump

```
CANCEL     START  0
           SAVE   (14,12)
           CANCEL
           END
```

Abend with dump

```
DUMP       START  0
           SAVE   (14,12)
           DUMP
           END
```

Figure 2-24   MVS and DOS/VSE assembler language subprograms for terminating a COBOL program

niques that you should use, you must also follow the specific guidelines
of your shop standards.

```
 PROCEDURE DIVISION.
*
 000-UPDATE-INVENTORY-FILE.
*
     OPEN INPUT   VALTRAN
          I-O     INVMAST
          OUTPUT ERRTRAN.
     IF INVMAST-ERROR-CODE NOT = '00'
         DISPLAY 'INV1300  A  1   OPEN ERROR FOR INVMAST'
         PERFORM 999-TERMINATE-UPDATE-PROGRAM.
     PERFORM 300-PROCESS-INVENTORY-TRAN
         UNTIL VALTRAN-EOF.
     CLOSE VALTRAN
           INVMAST
           ERRTRAN.
     IF INVMAST-ERROR-CODE NOT = '00'
         DISPLAY 'INV1300  A  5   CLOSE ERROR FOR INVMAST'
         PERFORM 999-TERMINATE-UPDATE-PROGRAM.
     DISPLAY 'INV1300   I  1   NORMAL EOJ'.
     STOP RUN.
*
 300-PROCESS-INVENTORY-TRAN.
*
     PERFORM 310-READ-INVENTORY-TRAN.
     IF NOT VALTRAN-EOF
         PERFORM 320-READ-INVENTORY-MASTER
         IF MASTER-FOUND
             PERFORM 330-UPDATE-INVENTORY-MASTER
             PERFORM 340-REWRITE-INVENTORY-MASTER
         ELSE
             PERFORM 350-WRITE-ERROR-TRAN.
*
 310-READ-INVENTORY-TRAN.
*
     READ VALTRAN INTO VALID-TRANSACTION-RECORD
         AT END
             MOVE 'Y' TO VALTRAN-EOF-SWITCH.
*
```

Figure 2-25   The random update program with improved error processing (part 1 of 2)

The random update program with improved error processing

Figure 2-25 shows a random update program with improved error
processing routines. Since this is the same update program I presented
in figure 2-18, I've only shown the Procedure Division here. In this
version, the program does a more complete job of error processing by
checking the FILE STATUS code after all I/O statements (OPEN,

```
 320-READ-INVENTORY-MASTER.
*
     MOVE IT-ITEM-NO TO MR-ITEM-NO.
     MOVE 'Y' TO MASTER-FOUND-SWITCH.
     READ INVMAST INTO INVENTORY-MASTER-RECORD.
     IF INVMAST-ERROR-CODE = '00'
         MOVE 'Y' TO MASTER-FOUND-SWITCH
     ELSE
         IF INVMAST-ERROR-CODE = '23'
             MOVE 'N' TO MASTER-FOUND-SWITCH
         ELSE
             DISPLAY 'INV1300 A 2   READ ERROR FOR INVMAST'
             DISPLAY 'INV1300 A 2   ITEM NUMBER = ' IM-ITEM-NO
             PERFORM 999-TERMINATE-UPDATE-PROGRAM.
*
 330-UPDATE-INVENTORY-MASTER.
*
     ADD IT-RECEIPT-QUANTITY TO IM-ON-HAND.
*
 340-REWRITE-INVENTORY-MASTER.
*
     REWRITE MASTER-RECORD-AREA FROM INVENTORY-MASTER-RECORD.
     IF INVMAST-ERROR-CODE NOT = '00'
         DISPLAY 'INV1300 A 3   REWRITE ERROR FOR INVMAST'
         DISPLAY 'INV1300 A 3   ITEM NUMBER = ' IM-ITEM-NO
         PERFORM 999-TERMINATE-UPDATE-PROGRAM.
*
 350-WRITE-ERROR-TRAN.
*
     WRITE ERROR-TRANSACTION FROM VALID-TRANSACTION-RECORD.
*
 999-TERMINATE-UPDATE-PROGRAM.
*
     DISPLAY 'INV1300 A 4   FILE STATUS = ' INVMAST-ERROR-CODE.
     DISPLAY 'INV1300 A 4   PROGRAM TERMINATED'.
     CALL 'DUMP'.
```

Figure 2-25   The random update program with improved error processing (part 2 of 2)

CLOSE, READ, and REWRITE). The new code is shaded in the source
listing. Keep in mind, though, that this program only provides error
checking for the INVMAST file. In a production environment, it would
probably provide error checking for the VALTRAN and ERRTRAN files
too.

   If VSAM detects a serious error during any of the I/O operations,
the program performs module 999. This module displays the FILE
STATUS code and a message indicating that it will terminate the program. Then, the module uses this statement

```
CALL 'DUMP'
```

to invoke the assembler language subprogram that causes the abend. Control never returns to the COBOL program.

Unfortunately, this practice violates one of the basic rules of structured programming. That is, every called module should return to the module that called it. Although it's possible to write code that adheres to this rule, it's just not worth the effort to do so. Since unrecoverable error conditions are rare, you should call the abend subprogram from wherever the error occurs and not worry about returning to the calling module.

Should you add an abend module like module 999 in figure 2-25 to the structure chart for your program? Here again, it's just not worth the effort. In most shops, you can use a general module number like 999 or 9999 for this type of module and not take the time to add it to your chart.

Discussion

I hope by now that you're convinced of the need for VSAM error processing in your COBOL programs. If you don't test the FILE STATUS code after every I/O statement, major errors can go undetected. And the longer they go undetected, the more difficult they are to track down.

The programs in the remainder of this book only provide for minimal error checking, just as the programs in topic 2 of this chapter did. That way, you'll be able to concentrate on the new code that the programs demonstrate. Remember, though, that all of your programs should provide for the error checking that is prescribed by your shop standards.

Terminology

abend
abnormal termination
file contention

Objectives

1. Explain why error processing is so important in COBOL programs that process VSAM files.

2. Given a COBOL program that processes VSAM files, code the error-processing routines that meet the standards of your shop.

Topic 4   COBOL for key-sequenced data sets with alternate indexes

As you'll recall from the first topic in this chapter, alternate indexes let you access records in a key-sequenced data set by a field other than the primary key. In this topic, I'll present the COBOL code you need to know to process key-sequenced files using alternate indexes. First, I'll present the SELECT statement and the FILE STATUS codes for use with alternate keys. Then, I'll show you the code that's specific to sequential processing and the code that's specific to random processing.

Before I start, I want you to realize two things. First, most batch COBOL programs that process key-sequenced files do not use alternate indexes. So you may or may not need to know the material this topic presents. And second, you have to set up an alternate index using AMS before you can access it in a COBOL program. You'll learn how to do that in chapter 6.

The SELECT statement

When you use an alternate index to access a key-sequenced data set, you must specify the alternate index in the SELECT statement for the file. Figure 2-26 shows the format of this statement. As you can see, there's one new clause: the ALTERNATE RECORD KEY clause, which contains the WITH DUPLICATES phrase.

The ALTERNATE RECORD KEY clause specifies the name of an alternate key field for the file. All the fields you name as alternate keys must be coded in the record description for the file in the File Section along with the primary key. Since a file can have more than one alternate key, you can code an ALTERNATE RECORD KEY clause for each of them. However, you don't have to code the clause for every alternate key. You code it only for those keys that you're going to use in your program.

The WITH DUPLICATES phrase specifies whether the alternate key is unique or non-unique. If you code this clause, VSAM assumes the keys are non-unique, so it's possible for more than one record to have the same alternate key. If you omit this clause, VSAM assumes the keys are unique. You specify whether an alternate index has unique or non-unique keys when you define it with AMS. So be sure you code this clause so it agrees with the AMS definition.

```
SELECT file-name

   ASSIGN TO system-name

   ORGANIZATION IS INDEXED

                   ⎛SEQUENTIAL⎞
   [ACCESS MODE IS ⎨RANDOM    ⎬]
                   ⎝DYNAMIC   ⎠

   RECORD KEY IS data-name-1

   [ALTERNATE RECORD KEY IS data-name-2
        [WITH DUPLICATES]] ...

   [FILE STATUS IS data-name-3]
```

Figure 2-26   The SELECT statement for key-sequenced files with alternate keys

FILE STATUS codes

When you process records via an alternate key that allows duplicates, you may get FILE STATUS code 02 rather than 00, even though the I/O statement you issued executed successfully. If you refer back to figure 2-23, you can see that code 02 means that the I/O operation was completed successfully, but a duplicate key was detected. This status only results when WITH DUPLICATES has been specified for the key in question.

In many cases, this status code won't significantly affect the way you code your program. All you have to do is check for 02 as well as 00 to see if the statement was successful. In other cases, your program may need to take some special action when the 02 code is encountered.

When you issue a WRITE or REWRITE statement, you'll get the 02 code if a duplicate key exists for any of the alternate keys you named and coded the WITH DUPLICATES phrase for in the file's SELECT statement. This is a normal condition, so your program doesn't need to take special action because of it. Keep in mind, though, that if a WRITE or REWRITE statement tries to write a record with a duplicate key value for an alternate key that doesn't allow duplicates, the system returns FILE STATUS 22 rather than 02. This isn't a normal condition, so you need to handle the error accordingly.

When you issue a random READ statement using an alternate key, the record retrieved is the first record in the alternate index that has the key value you specify. If there are additional records with the same alternate key value, you'll get the 02 status code. Then, the only way to retrieve those additional records is to issue sequential READ statements.

When you issue a sequential READ statement using an alternate key that allows duplicates, VSAM returns the 02 status code if there is at least one more record in the file that has the same alternate key value. When you read the last or only record that has a particular alternate key value, VSAM returns status code 00.

To illustrate, suppose a file has three records with alternate key 10001. When you read the first record (by either a random or sequential READ statement), VSAM returns status code 02 because there are more records with the same alternate key. When you read the second record with a sequential READ statement, VSAM returns status code 02 again. But when you read the third record, VSAM returns status code 00 because there are no more records in the file with the same alternate key value.

Sequential processing

Sequential processing of a key-sequenced data set by an alternate key is similar to processing by a primary key. The only difference is that before you begin processing, you must specify the key you want to use. You do this by issuing a START statement.

The START statement　　The START statement for alternate indexes has the same format as in figure 2-6. Instead of specifying the primary key in the KEY clause, though, you specify the alternate key. Then the alternate key becomes the *key of reference*. That means subsequent I/O statements will access the file in alternate key sequence, not primary key sequence. For example, to begin processing a file of employee records along the alternate index that represents social security number, you code statements like these:

```
MOVE ZERO TO EM-SOCIAL-SECURITY-NUMBER.
START EMPMAST
    KEY NOT < EM-SOCIAL-SECURITY-NUMBER.
```

Then, the system positions the file at the record with the lowest social security number that is not less than zero. And subsequent sequential READ statements will retrieve records in sequence by social security number. To change the key of reference, code another START statement and specify a different key.

A sequential retrieval program   Figure 2-27 presents the program specifications for a program that prints a listing of a file of open item records. As you can see in the program overview, the open item file is indexed by invoice number, and it has one alternate index (customer number) with non-unique keys. Since the records are to be listed in customer number sequence, they must be retrieved by the alternate key. As a result, the file is started along the alternate index and is read sequentially. For each customer open item, a line is printed on the listing. After all the records for a customer have been processed, a customer total line is printed. And after all the records in the file have been processed, a grand total line is printed.

Figure 2-28 presents the structure chart for this program, and figure 2-29 shows the program listing. In the SELECT statement for OPENITM, I've coded an ALTERNATE RECORD KEY clause that specifies OI-CUSTOMER-NUMBER as the alternate key. Because there can be more than one open item for the same customer, I coded the WITH DUPLICATES clause for this file. Notice in the File Section that I defined both the primary key and the alternate key in the record description for the file.

Next, look at the definition of the FILE STATUS field for the open item file, OPENITM-ERROR-CODE, in working storage. I defined two 88 conditions here: LAST-CUSTOMER-INVOICE and DUPLICATE-KEY. When the file status is 00, LAST-CUSTOMER-INVOICE is turned on. When the code is 02, DUPLICATE-KEY is turned on. (Although I didn't use the DUPLICATE-KEY condition in this program, I included it to clarify what I was testing for.)

Now, look at the Procedure Division. To start the employee file along the alternate index, the program moves LOW-VALUE to the key field and issues the START statement in module 100. Because I specified the alternate key in the KEY clause, this START statement positions the file at the first record in the alternate index. Then, subsequent READ statements retrieve the records in alternate key sequence.

The program uses the LAST-CUSTOMER-INVOICE condition in the main processing module, module 300, to determine when it should print the total line for a customer. As I described earlier, VSAM returns code 02 after a READ statement if there are more records with the same alternate key. When there are no more records for the customer, however, VSAM returns status code 00. When that happens, LAST-CUSTOMER-INVOICE is turned on, and module 300 calls module 340 to print a total line for the customer.

This program illustrates how the FILE STATUS field can be used to control processing as well as error handling. If I hadn't used the FILE STATUS field, the program would have to read the first record for the next customer to know there aren't any more records for the current

Program:	AR1100 Prepare open item listing	Page: 1
Designer:	Mike Murach	Date: 09-03-86

Input/output specifications

File	Description	Use
OPENITM	Open item master file	Input
OILIST	Print file: Open item listing	Output

Process specifications

This program prints a listing of all records in the open item master file
(OPENITM). This file's primary index is invoice number. However, the
listing is to be printed in customer number sequence, so the file must be
accessed sequentially by its non-unique alternate key, customer number.

The program prints totals for each customer. At the end of the listing, it
prints grand totals.

The basic processing requirements are:

Start the open item file along the alternate key, customer number.

For each record in the file:

1. Read an open item record.

2. Print a report line on the listing.

3. Accumulate the customer and grand totals.

4. If the record is the last one for a customer, print a customer total
    line.

Print a grand total line.

Figure 2-27   The program specifications for a sequential retrieval program that uses non-unique alternate
keys (part 1 of 2)

The record layout for the open item file

```
01    OPEN-ITEM-RECORD.
*
      05   OI-INVOICE-NUMBER              PIC X(6).
      05   OI-INVOICE-DATE                PIC X(6).
      05   OI-CUSTOMER-NUMBER             PIC X(6).
      05   OI-INVOICE-AMOUNTS.
           10   OI-PRODUCT-TOTAL          PIC S9(5)V99.
           10   OI-SALES-TAX              PIC S9(5)V99.
           10   OI-FREIGHT                PIC S9(5)V99.
           10   OI-INVOICE-TOTAL          PIC S9(5)V99.
      05   OI-PAYMENT-CREDIT-DATA.
           10   OI-SUM-OF-PAYMENTS        PIC S9(5)V99.
           10   OI-SUM-OF-CREDITS         PIC S9(5)V99.
           10   OI-BALANCE-DUE            PIC S9(5)V99.
```

The print chart for the open item listing

Figure 2-27   The program specifications for a sequential retrieval program that uses non-unique alternate keys (part 2 of 2)

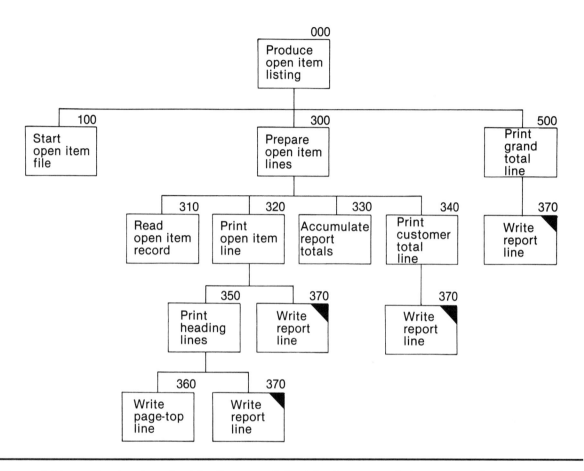

Figure 2-28 The structure chart for the sequential retrieval program that uses non-unique alternate keys

customer. This would require a control field to hold the last customer number and more complex code in the control module.

Random processing

To process a KSDS with an alternate index randomly, you code most I/O statements the same as you do for random processing by a primary key. Only the READ statement and the REWRITE statement are coded differently.

The READ statement Figure 2-30 shows the format of the READ statement for random processing of a KSDS with an alternate index.

```
 IDENTIFICATION DIVISION.
*
 PROGRAM-ID.  AR1100.
*
 ENVIRONMENT DIVISION.
*
 INPUT-OUTPUT SECTION.
*
 FILE-CONTROL.
     SELECT OPENITM  ASSIGN TO SYS020-OPENITM
                     ORGANIZATION IS INDEXED
                     ACCESS IS SEQUENTIAL
                     RECORD KEY IS OI-INVOICE-NUMBER
                     ALTERNATE RECORD KEY IS OI-CUSTOMER-NUMBER
                         WITH DUPLICATES
                     FILE STATUS IS OPENITM-ERROR-CODE.
     SELECT OILIST   ASSIGN TO SYS006-UR-1403-S.
*
 DATA DIVISION.
*
 FILE SECTION.
*
 FD  OPENITM
     LABEL RECORDS ARE STANDARD
     RECORD CONTAINS 67 CHARACTERS.
*
 01  OPEN-ITEM-RECORD.
*
     05  OI-INVOICE-NUMBER      PIC X(6).
     05  OI-INVOICE-DATE        PIC X(6).
     05  OI-CUSTOMER-NUMBER     PIC X(6).
     05  OI-INVOICE-AMOUNTS.
         10  OI-PRODUCT-TOTAL   PIC S9(5)V99.
         10  OI-SALES-TAX       PIC S9(5)V99.
         10  OI-FREIGHT         PIC S9(5)V99.
         10  OI-INVOICE-TOTAL   PIC S9(5)V99.
     05  OI-PAYMENT-CREDIT-DATA.
         10  OI-SUM-OF-PAYMENTS PIC S9(5)V99.
         10  OI-SUM-OF-CREDITS  PIC S9(5)V99.
         10  OI-BALANCE-DUE     PIC S9(5)V99.
*
 FD  OILIST
     LABEL RECORDS ARE OMITTED
     RECORD CONTAINS 132 CHARACTERS.
*
 01  PRINT-AREA             PIC X(132).
*
```

Figure 2-29   The sequential retrieval program that uses non-unique alternate keys (part 1 of 7)

```
WORKING-STORAGE SECTION.
*
 01   SWITCHES.
*
      05   OPENITM-EOF-SWITCH        PIC X    VALUE 'N'.
           88   OPENITM-EOF                   VALUE 'Y'.
      05   NEW-CUSTOMER-SWITCH       PIC X    VALUE 'Y'.
           88   NEW-CUSTOMER                  VALUE 'Y'.
*
 01   FILE-STATUS-FIELDS.
*
      05   OPENITM-ERROR-CODE        PIC XX.
           88   LAST-CUSTOMER-INVOICE         VALUE '00'.
           88   DUPLICATE-KEY                 VALUE '02'.
*
 01   PRINT-FIELDS                   COMP-3.
*
      05   SPACE-CONTROL             PIC S9.
      05   LINE-COUNT                PIC S9(3)     VALUE +99.
      05   LINES-ON-PAGE             PIC S9(3)     VALUE +55.
*
 01   TOTAL-FIELDS                   COMP-3.
*
      05   CUSTOMER-INVOICE-TOTAL    PIC S9(7)V99  VALUE ZERO.
      05   CUSTOMER-PAYMENTS         PIC S9(7)V99  VALUE ZERO.
      05   CUSTOMER-CREDITS          PIC S9(7)V99  VALUE ZERO.
      05   CUSTOMER-BALANCE-DUE      PIC S9(7)V99  VALUE ZERO.
      05   TOTAL-INVOICE-TOTAL       PIC S9(7)V99  VALUE ZERO.
      05   TOTAL-PAYMENTS            PIC S9(7)V99  VALUE ZERO.
      05   TOTAL-CREDITS             PIC S9(7)V99  VALUE ZERO.
      05   TOTAL-BALANCE-DUE         PIC S9(7)V99  VALUE ZERO.
*
 01   HEADING-LINE-1.
*
      05   FILLER    PIC X(20)   VALUE 'OPEN ITEM LISTING'.
      05   FILLER    PIC X(112)  VALUE SPACE.
*
 01   HEADING-LINE-2.
*
      05   FILLER    PIC X(20)   VALUE 'CUSTOMER   INVOICE    '.
      05   FILLER    PIC X(20)   VALUE '              INVOICE '.
      05   FILLER    PIC X(20)   VALUE '                     '.
      05   FILLER    PIC X(20)   VALUE '            BALANC'.
      05   FILLER    PIC X(20)   VALUE 'E                 '.
      05   FILLER    PIC X(32)   VALUE SPACE.
*
```

Figure 2-29   The sequential retrieval program that uses non-unique alternate keys (part 2 of 7)

```
 01   HEADING-LINE-3.
 *
      05   FILLER     PIC X(20)    VALUE ' NUMBER     NUMBER     '.
      05   FILLER     PIC X(20)    VALUE '               TOTAL   '.
      05   FILLER     PIC X(20)    VALUE '      PAYMENTS          '.
      05   FILLER     PIC X(20)    VALUE 'CREDITS             DU'.
      05   FILLER     PIC X(20)    VALUE 'E                      '.
      05   FILLER     PIC X(32)    VALUE SPACE.
 *
 01   INVOICE-LINE.
 *
      05   FILLER               PIC X           VALUE SPACE.
      05   IL-CUSTOMER-NUMBER   PIC X(6).
      05   FILLER               PIC X(3)        VALUE SPACE.
      05   IL-INVOICE-NUMBER    PIC X(6).
      05   FILLER               PIC X(14)       VALUE SPACE.
      05   IL-INVOICE-TOTAL     PIC ZZ,ZZ9.99-.
      05   FILLER               PIC X(4)        VALUE SPACE.
      05   IL-PAYMENTS          PIC ZZ,ZZ9.99-.
      05   FILLER               PIC X(4)        VALUE SPACE.
      05   IL-CREDITS           PIC ZZ,ZZ9.99-.
      05   FILLER               PIC X(4)        VALUE SPACE.
      05   IL-BALANCE-DUE       PIC ZZ,ZZ9.99-.
      05   FILLER               PIC X(50)       VALUE SPACE.
 *
 01   CUSTOMER-TOTAL-LINE.
 *
      05   FILLER               PIC X(10)       VALUE SPACE.
      05   FILLER               PIC X(19)
                                VALUE 'CUSTOMER TOTALS:'.
      05   CTL-INVOICE-TOTAL    PIC ZZZ,ZZ9.99-.
      05   FILLER               PIC X(3)        VALUE SPACE.
      05   CTL-PAYMENTS         PIC ZZZ,ZZ9.99-.
      05   FILLER               PIC X(3)        VALUE SPACE.
      05   CTL-CREDITS          PIC ZZZ,ZZ9.99-.
      05   FILLER               PIC X(3)        VALUE SPACE.
      05   CTL-BALANCE-DUE      PIC ZZZ,ZZ9.99-.
      05   FILLER               PIC X(50)       VALUE SPACE.
 *
```

Figure 2-29   The sequential retrieval program that uses non-unique alternate keys (part 3 of 7)

```
 01   GRAND-TOTAL-LINE.
*
     05    FILLER               PIC X(13)    VALUE SPACE.
     05    FILLER               PIC X(14)    VALUE 'GRAND TOTALS:'.
     05    GTL-INVOICE-TOTAL    PIC Z,ZZZ,ZZ9.99-.
     05    FILLER               PIC X        VALUE SPACE.
     05    GTL-PAYMENTS         PIC Z,ZZZ,ZZ9.99-.
     05    FILLER               PIC X        VALUE SPACE.
     05    GTL-CREDITS          PIC Z,ZZZ,ZZ9.99-.
     05    FILLER               PIC X        VALUE SPACE.
     05    GTL-BALANCE-DUE      PIC Z,ZZZ,ZZ9.99-.
     05    FILLER               PIC X(50)    VALUE SPACE.
*
 PROCEDURE DIVISION.
*
 000-PRODUCE-OPEN-ITEM-LISTING.
*
     OPEN INPUT  OPENITM
          OUTPUT OILIST.
     PERFORM 100-START-OPEN-ITEM-FILE.
     IF NOT OPENITM-EOF
         PERFORM 300-PREPARE-OPEN-ITEM-LINES
             UNTIL OPENITM-EOF
         PERFORM 500-PRINT-GRAND-TOTAL-LINE.
     CLOSE OPENITM
           OILIST.
     DISPLAY 'AR1100  I  1   NORMAL EOJ'.
     STOP RUN.
*
 100-START-OPEN-ITEM-FILE.
*
     MOVE LOW-VALUE TO OI-CUSTOMER-NUMBER.
     START OPENITM
         KEY IS NOT < OI-CUSTOMER-NUMBER.
     IF OPENITM-ERROR-CODE NOT = '00'
         DISPLAY 'AR1100  A  2   START ERROR FOR OPENITM'
         DISPLAY 'AR1100  A  2   FILE STATUS = '
             OPENITM-ERROR-CODE
         MOVE 'Y' TO OPENITM-EOF-SWITCH.
*
```

Figure 2-29   The sequential retrieval program that uses non-unique alternate keys (part 4 of 7)

```
 300-PREPARE-OPEN-ITEM-LINES.
*
     PERFORM 310-READ-OPEN-ITEM-RECORD.
     IF NOT OPENITM-EOF
         PERFORM 320-PRINT-OPEN-ITEM-LINE
         PERFORM 330-ACCUMULATE-REPORT-TOTALS
         IF LAST-CUSTOMER-INVOICE
             PERFORM 340-PRINT-CUSTOMER-TOTAL-LINE
             MOVE 'Y' TO NEW-CUSTOMER-SWITCH.
*
 310-READ-OPEN-ITEM-RECORD.
*
     READ OPENITM.
     IF        OPENITM-ERROR-CODE NOT = '00'
           AND OPENITM-ERROR-CODE NOT = '02'
         IF OPENITM-ERROR-CODE = '10'
             MOVE 'Y' TO OPENITM-EOF-SWITCH
         ELSE
             DISPLAY 'AR1100    A    3    READ ERROR FOR OPENITM'
             DISPLAY 'AR1100    A    3    CUSTOMER NUMBER = '
                 OI-CUSTOMER-NUMBER
             DISPLAY 'AR1100    A    3    FILE STATUS = '
                 OPENITM-ERROR-CODE
             MOVE 'Y' TO OPENITM-EOF-SWITCH.
*
 320-PRINT-OPEN-ITEM-LINE.
*
     IF LINE-COUNT > LINES-ON-PAGE
         PERFORM 350-PRINT-HEADING-LINES.
     IF NEW-CUSTOMER
         MOVE OI-CUSTOMER-NUMBER TO IL-CUSTOMER-NUMBER
         MOVE 'N' TO NEW-CUSTOMER-SWITCH
     ELSE
         MOVE SPACE TO IL-CUSTOMER-NUMBER.
     MOVE OI-INVOICE-NUMBER   TO IL-INVOICE-NUMBER.
     MOVE OI-INVOICE-TOTAL    TO IL-INVOICE-TOTAL.
     MOVE OI-SUM-OF-PAYMENTS  TO IL-PAYMENTS.
     MOVE OI-SUM-OF-CREDITS   TO IL-CREDITS.
     MOVE OI-BALANCE-DUE      TO IL-BALANCE-DUE.
     MOVE INVOICE-LINE        TO PRINT-AREA.
     PERFORM 370-WRITE-REPORT-LINE.
     MOVE 1 TO SPACE-CONTROL.
*
```

Figure 2-29   The sequential retrieval program that uses non-unique alternate keys (part 5 of 7)

```
330-ACCUMULATE-REPORT-TOTALS.
*
    ADD OI-INVOICE-TOTAL    TO CUSTOMER-INVOICE-TOTAL
                               TOTAL-INVOICE-TOTAL.
    ADD OI-SUM-OF-PAYMENTS  TO CUSTOMER-PAYMENTS
                               TOTAL-PAYMENTS.
    ADD OI-SUM-OF-CREDITS   TO CUSTOMER-CREDITS
                               TOTAL-CREDITS.
    ADD OI-BALANCE-DUE      TO CUSTOMER-BALANCE-DUE
                               TOTAL-BALANCE-DUE.
*
340-PRINT-CUSTOMER-TOTAL-LINE.
*
    MOVE CUSTOMER-INVOICE-TOTAL TO CTL-INVOICE-TOTAL.
    MOVE CUSTOMER-PAYMENTS      TO CTL-PAYMENTS.
    MOVE CUSTOMER-CREDITS       TO CTL-CREDITS.
    MOVE CUSTOMER-BALANCE-DUE   TO CTL-BALANCE-DUE.
    MOVE CUSTOMER-TOTAL-LINE    TO PRINT-AREA.
    MOVE 2 TO SPACE-CONTROL.
    PERFORM 370-WRITE-REPORT-LINE.
    MOVE ZERO TO CUSTOMER-INVOICE-TOTAL
                 CUSTOMER-PAYMENTS
                 CUSTOMER-CREDITS
                 CUSTOMER-BALANCE-DUE.
*
350-PRINT-HEADING-LINES.
*
    MOVE HEADING-LINE-1 TO PRINT-AREA.
    PERFORM 360-WRITE-PAGE-TOP-LINE.
    MOVE HEADING-LINE-2 TO PRINT-AREA.
    MOVE 2 TO SPACE-CONTROL.
    PERFORM 370-WRITE-REPORT-LINE.
    MOVE HEADING-LINE-3 TO PRINT-AREA.
    MOVE 1 TO SPACE-CONTROL.
    PERFORM 370-WRITE-REPORT-LINE.
    MOVE 2 TO SPACE-CONTROL.
*
360-WRITE-PAGE-TOP-LINE.
*
    WRITE PRINT-AREA AFTER ADVANCING PAGE.
    MOVE 1 TO LINE-COUNT.
*
```

Figure 2-29   The sequential retrieval program that uses non-unique alternate keys (part 6 of 7)

```
370-WRITE-REPORT-LINE.
*
    WRITE PRINT-AREA AFTER ADVANCING SPACE-CONTROL LINES.
    ADD SPACE-CONTROL TO LINE-COUNT.
*
500-PRINT-GRAND-TOTAL-LINE.
*
    MOVE TOTAL-INVOICE-TOTAL TO GTL-INVOICE-TOTAL.
    MOVE TOTAL-PAYMENTS      TO GTL-PAYMENTS.
    MOVE TOTAL-CREDITS       TO GTL-CREDITS.
    MOVE TOTAL-BALANCE-DUE   TO GTL-BALANCE-DUE.
    MOVE GRAND-TOTAL-LINE    TO PRINT-AREA.
    MOVE 3 TO SPACE-CONTROL.
    PERFORM 370-WRITE-REPORT-LINE.
```

Figure 2-29   The sequential retrieval program that uses non-unique alternate keys (part 7 of 7)

```
READ file-name RECORD
    [INTO identifier]
    KEY IS data-name
    [INVALID KEY imperative-statement]
```

Figure 2-30   The READ statement for random processing of key-sequenced files with alternate keys

The only new element here is the KEY clause. If you omit the KEY clause, your program uses the primary key as the key of reference. So when you read a KSDS randomly by alternate key, you must code the KEY clause in each READ statement to specify the alternate key as the key of reference.

The REWRITE statement   If you want to change the primary key of a record in a KSDS, you have to delete the existing record and write a new record with the new key. In contrast, if you want to change the alternate key of a record in a KSDS, you simply rewrite the record with the new key. Although you probably won't need to change an alternate key very often, it's good to know you can do it if you need to.

A random update program Figure 2-31 presents the program overview for a random update program. Its structure and logic are like the structure and logic of the random update program presented in the last topic: a transaction record is read and the associated master record is read and updated. The only difference is that this program retrieves records by an alternate key.

The master file used in this program is a file of employee records. The file is indexed by employee number, and it has two alternate keys: social security number and employee last name. The transactions used to update the master records don't contain the employee number, so the social security number must be used to access the records.

Figure 2-32 presents the source listing for this program. Notice I coded the ALTERNATE RECORD KEY clause without the WITH DUPLICATES phrase in the SELECT statement since the alternate key I'm using is unique. And because the program doesn't use the second alternate key (employee last name), I didn't specify it in the SELECT statement at all.

Also notice the READ statement for the master file in module 320. Here, the KEY clause specifies that the social security number field is the key of reference. Then, when the program issues the READ statement, it will try to read the record with the social security number that's stored in the alternate key field, MR-SOCIAL-SECURITY-NUMBER. If it can't find that record, VSAM returns FILE STATUS code 23 and the program turns the MASTER-FOUND-SWITCH off. If any other error condition occurs, the program turns the end-of-file switch on for the transaction file, which causes the program to end.

Discussion

There are both advantages and disadvantages to using alternate indexes. The main advantage is that they make it possible to retrieve records from a KSDS in a sequence other than that of the primary key without having to sort the file. Since sorting a large file can be time consuming, using alternate indexes can improve system efficiency. The main disadvantage of using alternate indexes is the extra time it takes to maintain these indexes as a file is processed. This reduces program efficiency. You have to decide for each application whether the advantages of using an alternate index outweigh the disadvantages.

Terminology

key of reference

Program:	PR1100 Update employee master file	Page: 1
Designer:	Mike Murach	Date: 09-03-86

Input/output specifications

File	Description	Use
EMPTRAN	Employee transaction file	Input
EMPMAST	Employee master file	Update
ERRTRAN	Error transaction file	Output

Process specifications

This program maintains the employee master file (EMPMAST) based on data in a file of valid employee transactions (EMPTRAN). The primary key of the master file is employee number. The file has two alternate keys: social security number, which is a unique key; and employee last name, which is a non-unique key.

Since the transaction file doesn't contain the employee number, the program accesses the master file using an alternate key, social security number. If a master record with the same social security number as the transaction isn't found, the program writes the transaction record in the error file. If a master record is found, the program uses the data in the transaction record to update the master record. If a field in the transaction record is non-blank, the value in the field moves to the corresponding field in the master record.

The basic processing requirements are:

1. Read a transaction record.

2. Read the related master record.

3. If the master record is found, update the master record.

4. If the master record isn't found, write a record on the file of error transactions.

Figure 2-31   The program overview for a random update program that uses unique alternate keys

```
 IDENTIFICATION DIVISION.
*
 PROGRAM-ID.  PR1100.
*
 ENVIRONMENT DIVISION.
*
 INPUT-OUTPUT SECTION.
*
 FILE-CONTROL.
     SELECT EMPTRAN   ASSIGN TO SYS020-AS-EMPTRAN.
     SELECT EMPMAST   ASSIGN TO SYS021-EMPMAST
                      ORGANIZATION IS INDEXED
                      ACCESS IS RANDOM
                      RECORD KEY IS MR-EMPLOYEE-NUMBER
                      ALTERNATE RECORD KEY
                          IS MR-SOCIAL-SECURITY-NUMBER
                      FILE STATUS IS EMPMAST-ERROR-CODE.
     SELECT ERRTRAN   ASSIGN TO SYS022-AS-ERRTRAN.
*
 DATA DIVISION.
*
 FILE SECTION.
*
 FD  EMPTRAN
     LABEL RECORDS ARE STANDARD
     RECORD CONTAINS 98 CHARACTERS.
*
 01  TRANSACTION-AREA          PIC X(98).
*
 FD  EMPMAST
     LABEL RECORDS ARE STANDARD
     RECORD CONTAINS 103 CHARACTERS.
*
 01  MASTER-RECORD-AREA.
*
     05  MR-EMPLOYEE-NUMBER           PIC X(5).
     05  FILLER                       PIC X(31).
     05  MR-SOCIAL-SECURITY-NUMBER    PIC X(9).
     05  FILLER                       PIC X(58).
*
 FD  ERRTRAN
     LABEL RECORDS ARE STANDARD
     RECORD CONTAINS 98 CHARACTERS.
*
 01  ERROR-TRANSACTION         PIC X(98).
*
```

Figure 2-32   The random update program that uses unique alternate keys (part 1 of 4)

```
WORKING-STORAGE SECTION.
*
01  SWITCHES.
*
    05  EMPTRAN-EOF-SWITCH      PIC X      VALUE 'N'.
        88  EMPTRAN-EOF                    VALUE 'Y'.
    05  MASTER-FOUND-SWITCH    PIC X.
        88  MASTER-FOUND                   VALUE 'Y'.
*
01  FILE-STATUS-FIELD.
*
    05  EMPMAST-ERROR-CODE     PIC XX.
*
01  EMPLOYEE-MAINTENANCE-TRAN.
*
    05  EMT-SOCIAL-SECURITY-NUMBER  PIC X(9).
    05  EMT-EMPLOYEE-NAME.
        10  EMT-FIRST-NAME         PIC X(10).
        10  EMT-INITIAL            PIC X.
        10  EMT-LAST-NAME          PIC X(20).
    05  EMT-ADDRESS                PIC X(30).
    05  EMT-CITY                   PIC X(21).
    05  EMT-STATE                  PIC XX.
    05  EMT-ZIP-CODE               PIC X(5).
*
01  EMPLOYEE-MASTER-RECORD.
*
    05  EMR-EMPLOYEE-NUMBER        PIC X(5).
    05  EMR-EMPLOYEE-NAME.
        10  EMR-FIRST-NAME         PIC X(10).
        10  EMR-INITIAL            PIC X.
        10  EMR-LAST-NAME          PIC X(20).
    05  EMR-SOCIAL-SECURITY-NUMBER  PIC X(9).
    05  EMR-ADDRESS                PIC X(30).
    05  EMR-CITY                   PIC X(21).
    05  EMR-STATE                  PIC XX.
    05  EMR-ZIP-CODE               PIC X(5).
*
```

Figure 2-32   The random update program that uses unique alternate keys (part 2 of 4)

Objective

Given specifications for a program that accesses an indexed file with one or more alternate indexes, code a COBOL solution.

```
PROCEDURE DIVISION.
*
 000-UPDATE-EMPLOYEE-FILE.
*
     OPEN INPUT  EMPTRAN
          I-O    EMPMAST
          EXTEND ERRTRAN.
     PERFORM 300-PROCESS-EMPLOYEE-TRAN
         UNTIL EMPTRAN-EOF.
     CLOSE EMPTRAN
           EMPMAST
           ERRTRAN.
     DISPLAY 'PR1100  I 1  NORMAL EOJ'.
     STOP RUN.
*
 300-PROCESS-EMPLOYEE-TRAN.
*
     PERFORM 310-READ-EMPLOYEE-TRAN.
     IF NOT EMPTRAN-EOF
         PERFORM 320-READ-EMPLOYEE-MASTER.
     IF NOT EMPTRAN-EOF
         IF MASTER-FOUND
             PERFORM 330-UPDATE-EMPLOYEE-MASTER
             PERFORM 340-REWRITE-EMPLOYEE-MASTER
         ELSE
             PERFORM 350-WRITE-ERROR-TRAN.
*
 310-READ-EMPLOYEE-TRAN.
*
     READ EMPTRAN INTO EMPLOYEE-MAINTENANCE-TRAN
         AT END
             MOVE 'Y' TO EMPTRAN-EOF-SWITCH.
*
```

Figure 2-32　　The random update program that uses unique alternate keys (part 3 of 4)

```
320-READ-EMPLOYEE-MASTER.
*
    MOVE EMT-SOCIAL-SECURITY-NUMBER
        TO MR-SOCIAL-SECURITY-NUMBER.
    MOVE 'Y' TO MASTER-FOUND-SWITCH.
    READ EMPMAST INTO EMPLOYEE-MASTER-RECORD
        KEY IS MR-SOCIAL-SECURITY-NUMBER.
    IF EMPMAST-ERROR-CODE NOT = '00'
        IF EMPMAST-ERROR-CODE = '23'
            MOVE 'N' TO MASTER-FOUND-SWITCH
        ELSE
            DISPLAY 'PR1100  A  2  READ ERROR FOR EMPMAST'
            DISPLAY 'PR1100  A  2  SOC SEC NUMBER = '
                EMT-SOCIAL-SECURITY-NUMBER
            DISPLAY 'PR1100  A  2  FILE STATUS = '
                EMPMAST-ERROR-CODE
            MOVE 'Y' TO EMPTRAN-EOF-SWITCH.
*
330-UPDATE-EMPLOYEE-MASTER.
*
    IF EMT-FIRST-NAME NOT EQUAL SPACE
        MOVE EMT-FIRST-NAME TO EMR-FIRST-NAME.
    IF EMT-INITIAL NOT EQUAL SPACE
        MOVE EMT-INITIAL TO EMR-INITIAL.
    IF EMT-LAST-NAME NOT EQUAL SPACE
        MOVE EMT-LAST-NAME TO EMR-LAST-NAME.
    IF EMT-ADDRESS NOT EQUAL SPACE
        MOVE EMT-ADDRESS TO EMR-ADDRESS.
    IF EMT-CITY NOT EQUAL SPACE
        MOVE EMT-CITY TO EMR-CITY.
    IF EMT-STATE NOT EQUAL SPACE
        MOVE EMT-STATE TO EMR-STATE.
    IF EMT-ZIP-CODE NOT EQUAL SPACE
        MOVE EMT-ZIP-CODE TO EMR-ZIP-CODE.
*
340-REWRITE-EMPLOYEE-MASTER.
*
    REWRITE MASTER-RECORD-AREA FROM EMPLOYEE-MASTER-RECORD.
    IF EMPMAST-ERROR-CODE NOT = '00'
        DISPLAY 'PR1100  A  3  REWRITE ERROR FOR EMPMAST'
        DISPLAY 'PR1100  A  3  SOC SEC NUMBER = '
            MR-SOCIAL-SECURITY-NUMBER
        DISPLAY 'PR1100  A  3  FILE STATUS = '
            EMPMAST-ERROR-CODE
        MOVE 'Y' TO EMPTRAN-EOF-SWITCH.
*
350-WRITE-ERROR-TRAN.
*
    WRITE ERROR-TRANSACTION FROM EMPLOYEE-MAINTENANCE-TRAN.
```

Figure 2-32   The random update program that uses unique alternate keys (part 4 of 4)

Topic 5   VS COBOL II for key-sequenced data sets

VS COBOL II is IBM's latest COBOL compiler for MVS systems. IBM developed VS COBOL II as a replacement for its older VS COBOL compiler, which was based on standards adopted by the American National Standards Institute (ANSI) in 1974. The VS COBOL II compiler is based on new standards adopted by ANSI in 1985. Although the VS COBOL II compiler provides many enhancements, only a few of the changes relate to VSAM file handling.

Figure 2-33 presents the COBOL elements you use for processing a KSDS. In this topic, I'll describe the new features for VSAM file handling, which are shaded in figure 2-33.

The VSAM-code field

If you look at figure 2-33, you'll see that the FILE STATUS clause has been expanded. Now, in addition to the file status field, you can specify a second field, called the *VSAM-code* field. The VSAM-code field provides additional information about the completion status of VSAM I/O operations. For most programs, the file status field provides all the information you need to handle VSAM errors properly. If you need more information, though, it's available in the VSAM-code field.

If you use the VSAM-code field, you must define it in working-storage as a six-byte group item, as shown in figure 2-34. As you can see, VSAM uses the first two bytes of this field for a *VSAM return code*, the second two bytes for a *VSAM function code*, and the last two bytes for a *VSAM feedback code*. When an error occurs during an I/O request for a file, VSAM places the appropriate codes in these areas. Then, you can test this field and take whatever action is necessary.

The VSAM return code contains information similar to that in the FILE STATUS code. Figure 2-35 presents the possible VSAM return codes and their meanings. As you can see, a return code of 0 indicates the request was successful. A return code of 4 indicates the request was unsuccessful because an I/O request was already pending for the same file. A return code of 8 indicates a logical error. And a return code of 12 indicates a physical error. Although the same information is available in the FILE STATUS code, the VSAM return code is important because it determines the possible values of the VSAM function code and the VSAM feedback code.

SELECT statement

```
SELECT file-name

    ASSIGN TO system-name
    ORGANIZATION IS INDEXED

                        (SEQUENTIAL)
    [ACCESS MODE IS    { RANDOM     }]
                        (DYNAMIC    )

    RECORD KEY IS data-name-1

    [ALTERNATE RECORD KEY IS data-name-2
        [WITH DUPLICATES]] ...

    [FILE STATUS IS data-name-3 [vsam-code]]
```

Note: The RECORD KEY field must be defined in the File Section as a field within the record description. The data-name-3 field in the FILE STATUS clause must be defined in working storage as a two-byte alphanumeric item. The vsam-code field in the FILE STATUS clause must be defined in working storage as a six-byte group item.

FD statement

```
FD  file-name
    [LABEL RECORDS ARE STANDARD]
    [RECORD CONTAINS integer CHARACTERS]
```

Procedure Division statements

```
                            (EQUAL TO                    )
                            (=                            )
                            (GREATER THAN                 )
                            (>                            )
START file-name [KEY IS    { NOT LESS THAN                } data-name]
                            (NOT <                         )
                            (GREATER THAN OR EQUAL TO      )
                            (>=                            )

    [INVALID KEY imperative-statement-1]
    [NOT INVALID KEY imperative-statement-2]
    [END-START]
```

Figure 2-33   VS COBOL II elements for processing key-sequenced files (part 1 of 2)

Sequential READ statement

```
READ file-name [NEXT] RECORD
    [INTO identifier]
    [AT END imperative-statement-1]
    [NOT AT END imperative-statement-2]
    [END-READ]
```

Random READ statement

```
READ file-name RECORD
    [INTO identifier]
    [KEY IS data-name]
    [INVALID KEY imperative-statement-1]
    [NOT INVALID KEY imperative-statement-2]
    [END-READ]
```

```
WRITE record-name
    [FROM identifier]
    [INVALID KEY imperative-statement-1]
    [NOT INVALID KEY imperative-statement-2]
    [END-WRITE]
```

```
REWRITE record-name
    [FROM identifier]
    [INVALID KEY imperative-statement-1]
    [NOT INVALID KEY imperative-statement-2]
    [END-REWRITE]
```

```
DELETE file-name RECORD
    [INVALID KEY imperative-statement-1]
    [NOT INVALID KEY imperative-statement-2]
    [END-DELETE]
```

Note: The new features for VS COBOL II are shaded.

Figure 2-33   VS COBOL II elements for processing key-sequenced files (part 2 of 2)

If the VSAM return code is 8 or 12, indicating that a logical or physical error occurred, the VSAM function code indicates the function you were attempting. Figure 2-36 presents these function codes and their meanings.

```
01  VSAM-CODE-FIELD              COMP.
*
    05  VSAM-RETURN-CODE         PIC 99.
    05  VSAM-FUNCTION-CODE       PIC 99
    05  VSAM-FEEDBACK-CODE       PIC 99.
```

Figure 2-34   Format of the VSAM-code field

Code	Explanation
0	The request has been successfully completed.
4	A request is already active for the file specified.
8	A logical error has occurred; check the feedback code for specific information.
12	A physical error has occurred; check the feedback code for specific information.

Figure 2-35   VSAM return codes

Figure 2-36 also has a column that displays the status of the *upgrade set* for each VSAM code. As you'll learn in chapter 6, an upgrade set consists of all of a base cluster's upgradable alternate indexes. So if you're processing a KSDS that doesn't have an upgradable alternate index, you don't need to worry about the values in this column. But if you're processing a KSDS that does have an upgradable alternate index and your program detects an I/O error and returns a VSAM function code of 1, 3, or 5, you should use AMS to rebuild the alternate index. That's the only way you can be sure the index will be correct. I'll show you how to do that in chapter 6.

The VSAM feedback code gives more specific information about the I/O error. For example, if the system detects a logical error, a feedback code of 96 means you attempted to change the key of reference while updating a record. And a feedback code of 68 means the OPEN statement you specified for the file doesn't allow the type of processing you attempted. Because so many different error codes are possible, I won't try to list them all here. If you need to find out what they are, you can refer to the *OS/VS VSAM Programmer's Guide*.

Code	Explanation	Status of upgrade set
0	An attempt was made to access a base cluster.	Correct
1	An attempt was made to access a base cluster.	May be incorrect
2	An attempt was made to access an alternate index of a base cluster.	Correct
3	An attempt was made to access an alternate index of a base cluster.	May be incorrect
4	An attempt was made to update the upgrade set for a base cluster.	Correct
5	An attempt was made to update the upgrade set for a base cluster.	May be incorrect

Figure 2-36   VSAM function codes

The FD statement

Using VS COBOL II, the only difference in the FD statement is that the LABEL RECORDS ARE STANDARD clause is optional. And since the label records are always standard, you may as well omit the clause.

Procedure Division elements

The START statement When you issue a START statement in VS COBOL, you can use any one of three relational operators: equal to, greater than, or not less than. But, as you can see in figure 2-33, VS COBOL II also gives you the option of using a greater-than-or-equal-to operator. Figure 2-37 shows how this can affect your coding. As you can see, using greater than or equal to makes the condition a little easier to understand.

START statement without using greater-than-or-equal-to

```
MOVE 1000 TO IM-ITEM-NUMBER.
START INVMAST KEY IS NOT < IM-ITEM-NUMBER
    INVALID KEY
        MOVE 'N' TO RECORD-FOUND-SWITCH.
```

START statement using greater-than-or-equal-to

```
MOVE 1000 TO IM-ITEM-NUMBER.
START INVMAST KEY IS >= IM-ITEM-NUMBER
    INVALID KEY
        MOVE 'N' TO RECORD-FOUND-SWITCH.
```

Figure 2-37 How the greater-than-or-equal-to condition can improve the readability of a START statement

Structured delimiters Figure 2-38 shows the I/O verbs that have *structured delimiters* under VS COBOL II. Simply stated, the purpose of a structured delimiter is to show where a statement ends. So in the example in figure 2-38, the READ statement ends with the END-READ delimiter. However, the IF condition is still in effect for the MOVE statement that follows.

In general, structured delimiters are only useful when one conditional statement is used within another one, as in the example in figure 2-38. If a statement isn't used within another statement, it doesn't need a structured delimiter because the period at the end of the statement is the delimiter. As a result, structured delimiters should have only a minor effect on your coding and little or no effect on the way you design programs.

If you isolate I/O statements in their own modules, and if you avoid the use of the AT END and INVALID KEY clauses, you won't ever need delimiters for I/O statements. That's why none of the programs in this book would benefit from the use of delimiters. As a general rule, then, you shouldn't need structured delimiters on I/O statements for VSAM files.

NOT clauses Many COBOL statements provide clauses for specific conditions like the AT END condition in a sequential READ statement or the INVALID KEY clause in a random READ statement. Under the VS COBOL II compiler , these statements also provide a clause that is executed when the condition doesn't occur. For instance, you can code a

Input/output verbs

READ	REWRITE	WRITE
DELETE	START	

Example

```
IF CONDITION-A
    READ VALTRAN NEXT RECORD
        AT END
            MOVE 'Y' TO VALTRAN-EOF-SWITCH
    END-READ
    MOVE IT-ITEM-NO TO OLD-ITEM-NO.
```

Figure 2-38   I/O verb list for structured delimiters

NOT AT END clause in a sequential READ statement or a NOT INVALID KEY clause in a random READ statement.

As I explained in topic 3, you shouldn't use the AT END or INVALID KEY clauses for VSAM files if you want to do a complete job of error processing. That's why you probably won't have much use for them.

Discussion

In this topic, I haven't presented all of the new code available under VS COBOL II. Instead, I've presented only those elements that relate to VSAM file processing. If you'd like to learn more about VS COBOL II, I recommend *VS COBOL II* by Anne Prince.

Terminology

VSAM code	VSAM feedback code
VSAM return code	upgrade set
VSAM function code	structured delimiter

Objective

Given a complete COBOL program that processes VSAM files, make modifications to the program so it uses the appropriate VS COBOL II elements presented in this topic.

Chapter 3

COBOL for entry-sequenced data sets

If you know how to use non-VSAM sequential files, you don't have to learn much to use VSAM entry-sequenced data sets. In fact, all of the sequential files in the last chapter were VSAM data sets. If you didn't notice that, it's because the code for an ESDS is so similar to the code for a non-VSAM sequential file.

The coding and logic for an ESDS is also much the same as the coding and logic for a KSDS that is processed sequentially. As a result, the Procedure Division for the sequential update program in figure 2-12 is the same when the master file is an ESDS as it is when the master file is a KSDS. That's why I won't spend much time on the code for entry-sequenced data sets.

COBOL elements for entry-sequenced data sets

Figure 3-1 summarizes the COBOL elements used to process entry-sequenced files. After I introduce these statements, I'll present a sample program to show you how they're used.

Note that I included the VS COBOL II elements in figure 3-1. However, since the VS COBOL II elements are the same for entry-sequenced data sets as they are for key-sequenced data sets processed sequentially, I won't mention them in this chapter. If you have any questions about them, please refer to topic 5 in chapter 2.

The SELECT statement   Figure 3-2 presents the format for system names for entry-sequenced files on both DOS/VSE and MVS systems. Note that "AS-" must appear in each system-name before the name or

SELECT statement

```
SELECT file-name
    ASSIGN TO system-name
    [ORGANIZATION IS SEQUENTIAL]
    [ACCESS MODE IS SEQUENTIAL]
    [FILE STATUS IS data-name [vsam-code]]
```

FD statement

```
FD  file-name
    [LABEL RECORDS ARE STANDARD]
    [RECORD CONTAINS integer CHARACTERS]
```

Procedure Division statements

```
      ⎧INPUT   file-name-1 ...⎫
OPEN  ⎪OUTPUT  file-name-2 ...⎪  ...
      ⎨I-O     file-name-3 ...⎬
      ⎩EXTEND  file-name-4 ...⎭
```

```
READ file-name [NEXT] RECORD
    [INTO data-name]
    [AT END imperative-statement-1]
    [NOT AT END imperative-statement-2]
    [END-READ]
```

```
WRITE record-name
    [FROM data-name]
    [END-WRITE]
```

```
REWRITE record-name
    [FROM data-name]
    [END-REWRITE]
```

```
CLOSE file-name ...
```

Note: The new features for VS COBOL II are shaded.

Figure 3-1   COBOL elements for processing entry-sequenced data sets

VS COBOL on a DOS/VSE system

Format: `SYSnnn-[comments-]AS-name`

Example: `SYS020-AS-INVMAST`

Notes: 1.   The SYS number is a number between SYS000 and SYS240 that is used to identify a specific I/O device. Find out what numbers you should use on your system.

2.   The *name* consists of from three to seven letters or digits, starting with a letter. For consistency, this can be the same name as the file name. This name is used in the JCL for running the program to relate the file description in the program with a file on disk.

VS COBOL or VS COBOL II on an MVS system

Format: `[comment-]AS-ddname`

Example: `AS-INVMAST`

Notes: The *ddname* is made up of eight or fewer letters or digits, starting with a letter. For consistency, this name can be the same as the file name. This name is used in the JCL for running the program to relate the file description in the program with a file on disk.

Figure 3-2   The formats of system names for entry-sequenced files

ddname. Other than that, the format for system-names is the same for entry-sequenced data sets as it is for key-sequenced data sets.

When you process an ESDS, you specify SEQUENTIAL in both the ORGANIZATION and ACCESS clauses in the SELECT statement. Since both of these clauses will default to SEQUENTIAL if you don't code them, they are optional for entry-sequenced files. But I recommend you code them anyway. That way, it's obvious that the file is an ESDS.

The FILE STATUS clause for an ESDS operates just as it does for other types of VSAM files. The return codes you'll see most often are 00 (operation successful) and 10 (end of file). If the system returns any other code, you should terminate the program and find out what caused the problem.

No BLOCK CONTAINS clause in the FD statement   If you've used non-VSAM sequential files, you know that you usually code a BLOCK CONTAINS clause in the FD statement. If you look in figure 3-1, though, you'll see that I didn't include this clause in the ESDS summary. Although you can code it for an ESDS, the compiler treats it as a comment because the COBOL program doesn't determine how many records are going to be stored in each control interval. That's done outside of the program.

The OPEN EXTEND statement   An option that's available for VSAM entry-sequenced files is the EXTEND option of the OPEN statement, as in this example:

```
OPEN INPUT   ORDERS
     EXTEND  INVTRANS.
```

You can use the EXTEND option when you want to add records to a file during either a creation or an update run. When the program opens the file, it automatically moves past the records already stored and adds the new record to the end of the file. In other words, the entire file doesn't have to be read before the additions can be made. (This is the same as coding DISP = MOD on the DD statement for a standard sequential file on an MVS system.) The only I/O verb that can be used for a file when it's opened as EXTEND is WRITE.

An edit program that extends an ESDS

Figure 3-3 gives a program overview for a simple edit program. This program reads a sequential file of inventory transactions; it produces a sequential file of valid transactions and another sequential file of invalid transactions. Note, though, that the file of valid transactions is to be extended. This means the VALTRAN file already exists and the program should add the valid records to it after the last record in the file. In contrast, the error transaction file is an output file so it will be created by the program.

This program is unrealistic, of course, because it has been simplified for illustrative purposes. As a result, the transaction record is short and only a limited amount of validity checking is required. Also, the program just writes the invalid records on the file of error transactions. In practice, an edit program often prints a listing of invalid records so they can be corrected and processed later on.

Figure 3-4 presents the structure chart for this program. It consists of only six modules. The two we'll concentrate on are modules 330 and 340, which contain the WRITE statements for the files.

Figure 3-5 presents the source code for this program. If you check the SELECT statements for the valid transaction file and the error transaction file, you can see that they are defined with FILE STATUS fields named VALTRAN-ERROR-CODE and ERRTRAN-ERROR-CODE.

In module 330, you can see the WRITE statement for the valid transaction file. The IF statement that follows it checks the FILE STATUS

Program: INV2100 Edit inventory transactions	Page: 1
Designer: Mike Murach	Date: 09-03-86

Input/output specifications

File	Description	Use
INVTRAN	Inventory transaction file	Input
VALTRAN	Valid inventory transaction file	Extend
ERRTRAN	Invalid inventory transaction file	Output

Process specifications

This program edits a file of inventory transactions (INVTRAN). If all of
the fields in a transaction are valid using the editing rules below, the
record is valid. Then, the program writes the record in the valid
transaction file (VALTRAN). But if one or more fields is invalid, the
record is invalid. Then, the program writes the record in the invalid
transaction file (ERRTRAN). The format of the records in all three
transaction files is the same.

The basic processing requirements are:

1. Read a transaction record.

2. Edit the fields in the record.

3. If the record is valid, write the record in the valid transaction file.

4. If the record is invalid, write the record in the invalid transaction
    file.

Editing rules:

IT-ITEM-NO	Must be numeric
IT-VENDOR-NO	Must be numeric
IT-RECEIPT-QUANTITY	Must be numeric

Figure 3-3   The program overview for an edit program that extends a sequential file of valid transactions

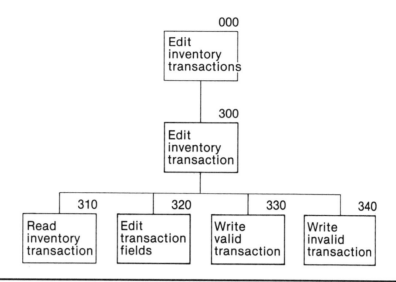

Figure 3-4 The structure chart for the sequential edit program

field to see how the WRITE operation turned out. If the FILE STATUS field has a value of 00, it means the operation was successful, so the program continues. However, if the file status value is anything other than 00, a message is displayed and the end-of-file switch for the input file is turned on so the program will end.

Similarly, in module 340, you can see the WRITE statement for the error transaction file. After this statement, the FILE STATUS field is checked to make sure the operation was successful. If it wasn't, an error message is displayed and INVTRAN-EOF-SWITCH is turned on so the program will end before another transaction is read.

Discussion

I haven't gone into too much detail in this chapter, because VSAM entry-sequenced data sets aren't used much. One reason for this is that VSAM doesn't provide much of an improvement over the other sequential access methods in terms of efficiency. A second, and more important, reason is that ESDS processing is more limited than non-VSAM sequential file processing. For example, VSAM doesn't provide for automatic handling of generation data sets, and that's essential for many sequential applications. Perhaps IBM will correct these problems someday. Until then, entry-sequenced VSAM files will be used infrequently.

```
 IDENTIFICATION DIVISION.
*
 PROGRAM-ID.  INV2100.
*
 ENVIRONMENT DIVISION.
*
 INPUT-OUTPUT SECTION.
*
 FILE-CONTROL.
     SELECT INVTRAN    ASSIGN TO SYS020-AS-INVTRAN.
     SELECT VALTRAN    ASSIGN TO SYS021-AS-VALTRAN
                       ORGANIZATION IS SEQUENTIAL
                       ACCESS IS SEQUENTIAL
                       FILE STATUS IS VALTRAN-ERROR-CODE.
     SELECT ERRTRAN    ASSIGN TO SYS022-AS-ERRTRAN
                       ORGANIZATION IS SEQUENTIAL
                       ACCESS IS SEQUENTIAL
                       FILE STATUS IS ERRTRAN-ERROR-CODE.
*
 DATA DIVISION.
*
 FILE SECTION.
*
 FD  INVTRAN
     LABEL RECORDS ARE STANDARD
     RECORD CONTAINS 21 CHARACTERS.
*
 01  INVENTORY-TRANSACTION.
*
     05  IT-ITEM-NO          PIC X(5).
     05  IT-VENDOR-NO        PIC X(5).
     05  IT-RECEIPT-DATE     PIC X(6).
     05  IT-RECEIPT-QUANTITY PIC X(5).
*
 FD  VALTRAN
     LABEL RECORDS ARE STANDARD
     RECORD CONTAINS 21 CHARACTERS.
*
 01  VALID-TRANSACTION       PIC X(21).
*
 FD  ERRTRAN
     LABEL RECORDS ARE STANDARD
     RECORD CONTAINS 21 CHARACTERS.
*
 01  ERROR-TRANSACTION       PIC X(21).
*
```

Figure 3-5   The sequential edit program (part 1 of 3)

```
 WORKING-STORAGE SECTION.
 *
 01   SWITCHES.
 *
      05   INVTRAN-EOF-SWITCH      PIC X    VALUE 'N'.
           88   INVTRAN-EOF                 VALUE 'Y'.
      05   VALID-TRAN-SWITCH       PIC X.
           88   VALID-TRAN                  VALUE 'Y'.
 *
 01   FILE-STATUS-FIELDS.
 *
      05   VALTRAN-ERROR-CODE      PIC XX.
      05   ERRTRAN-ERROR-CODE      PIC XX.
 *
 PROCEDURE DIVISION.
 *
 000-EDIT-INVENTORY-TRANS.
 *
      OPEN INPUT   INVTRAN
           EXTEND VALTRAN
           OUTPUT ERRTRAN.
      PERFORM 300-EDIT-INVENTORY-TRAN
          UNTIL INVTRAN-EOF.
      CLOSE INVTRAN
            VALTRAN
            ERRTRAN.
      DISPLAY 'INV2100  I  1  NORMAL EOJ'.
      STOP RUN.
 *
 300-EDIT-INVENTORY-TRAN.
 *
      PERFORM 310-READ-INVENTORY-TRAN.
      IF NOT INVTRAN-EOF
          PERFORM 320-EDIT-TRANSACTION-FIELDS
          IF VALID-TRAN
              PERFORM 330-WRITE-VALID-TRAN
          ELSE
              PERFORM 340-WRITE-INVALID-TRAN.
 *
 310-READ-INVENTORY-TRAN.
 *
      READ INVTRAN
          AT END
              MOVE 'Y' TO INVTRAN-EOF-SWITCH.
 *
```

Figure 3-5   The sequential edit program (part 2 of 3)

```
 320-EDIT-TRANSACTION-FIELDS.
*
     MOVE 'Y' TO VALID-TRAN-SWITCH.
     IF       IT-ITEM-NO NOT NUMERIC
         OR IT-VENDOR-NO NOT NUMERIC
         OR IT-RECEIPT-QUANTITY NOT NUMERIC
        MOVE 'N' TO VALID-TRAN-SWITCH.
*
 330-WRITE-VALID-TRAN.
*
     WRITE VALID-TRANSACTION FROM INVENTORY-TRANSACTION.
     IF VALTRAN-ERROR-CODE NOT = '00'
         DISPLAY 'INV2100  A  2  WRITE ERROR FOR VALTRAN'
         DISPLAY 'INV2100  A  2  ITEM NUMBER = ' IT-ITEM-NO
         DISPLAY 'INV2100  A  2  FILE STATUS = '
             VALTRAN-ERROR-CODE
         MOVE 'Y' TO INVTRAN-EOF-SWITCH.
*
 340-WRITE-INVALID-TRAN.
*
     WRITE ERROR-TRANSACTION FROM INVENTORY-TRANSACTION.
     IF ERRTRAN-ERROR-CODE NOT = '00'
         DISPLAY 'INV2100  A  3  WRITE ERROR FOR ERRTRAN'
         DISPLAY 'INV2100  A  3  ITEM NUMBER = ' IT-ITEM-NO
         DISPLAY 'INV2100  A  3  FILE STATUS = '
             ERRTRAN-ERROR-CODE
         MOVE 'Y' TO INVTRAN-EOF-SWITCH.
```

Figure 3-5   The sequential edit program (part 3 of 3)

Objective

Given the specifications for a program using VSAM entry-sequenced
files, code a COBOL solution.

Chapter 4

COBOL for relative record data sets

A relative record data set consists of a specified number of areas. Each of these areas, called a *slot*, can contain one record and is identified by a *relative record number*, or *RRN*, that indicates its relative position in the file. For example, the record in the first slot in an RRDS is identified by relative record number 1 and the record in the tenth slot in the file is identified by relative record number 10, whether or not slots 2 through 9 contain records. It's important to distinguish between the slots and the records; the relative record numbers identify the slots, not the records. To access records in an RRDS, you use these relative record numbers.

Like a record in a key-sequenced file, a record in a relative record file can be accessed both sequentially and randomly. Unlike a key-sequenced file, however, a relative record file doesn't have an index. Instead, relative organization depends on a direct relationship between the data in each record and its relative position in the file.

In some applications, you can use a field in the record as the relative record number. In others, you can convert a field like employee number to a value that's acceptable as an RRN. Often, though, there's no apparent relationship between the key fields in the records and acceptable RRNs. As a result, relative record files aren't used very often.

Because relative record files are useful in some applications, I'll show you how to use them in this chapter. First, I'll show you the code for sequential processing; then, the code for random processing; last, the code for dynamic processing. Since the logic and coding for relative record data sets is so similar to that used for key-sequenced data sets,

103

I'll cover only the elements that are unique to relative record files in this chapter.

As you will see, I included the VS COBOL II elements in the COBOL summaries for relative record data sets in this chapter. For the most part, the VS COBOL II elements are the same for relative record data sets as they are for key-sequenced data sets. If you have any questions about them, please refer to topic 5 in chapter 2.

Sequential processing

Figure 4-1 shows the COBOL elements you use when you process an RRDS sequentially. Most of these elements are the same as the elements you use when you process a KSDS sequentially. However, there are a couple of differences that you should be aware of.

The SELECT statement   When you're processing an RRDS, you must specify ORGANIZATION IS RELATIVE in the SELECT statement. Then, when you're processing the RRDS sequentially, you code ACCESS IS SEQUENTIAL.

The RELATIVE KEY clause in the SELECT statement specifies a numeric field that will contain the relative record number for a record in the file. For sequential processing, though, this clause is optional. You only need to code it if you're going to use a START statement.

If you use the RELATIVE KEY clause, you shouldn't define the field in the file's record description in the File Section. Instead, you must define it in working storage as an unsigned numeric field. Even if you use a field in the record as the relative record number, the RELATIVE KEY clause can't refer to a field in the record description in the File Section.

The FILE STATUS clause operates just as it does for other types of VSAM files. Figure 4-2 shows the FILE STATUS codes you'll see most often when you process relative record files.

The OPEN statement   Note in figure 4-1 that the EXTEND option is shaded, indicating that it is a part of the 1985 COBOL standards. In the 1974 standards, a relative file couldn't be opened in extend mode. However, the EXTEND option can only be used if the file is opened for sequential access; it can't be specified if the file is opened for dynamic access, even if the file is only accessed sequentially.

The READ statement   Although the READ statement has the same format for accessing relative files sequentially as it does for accessing sequential files, there is one point I would like to make. As I mentioned, there may be empty record slots in an RRDS. Then, when you're

SELECT statement

```
SELECT file-name
    ASSIGN TO system-name
    ORGANIZATION IS RELATIVE
    [ACCESS MODE IS SEQUENTIAL]
    [RELATIVE KEY IS data-name-1]
    [FILE STATUS IS data-name-2 [vsam-code]]
```

Note: Both the RELATIVE KEY field and the FILE STATUS field must be defined in
        working storage.

FD statement

```
FD  file-name
    [LABEL RECORDS ARE STANDARD]
    [RECORD CONTAINS integer CHARACTERS]
```

Procedure Division statements

```
      ⎧ INPUT   file-name-1 ... ⎫
OPEN  ⎪ OUTPUT  file-name-2 ... ⎪
      ⎨ I-O     file-name-3 ... ⎬
      ⎩ EXTEND  file-name-4 ... ⎭
```

```
                            ⎧ EQUAL TO                    ⎫
                            ⎪ =                           ⎪
                            ⎪ GREATER THAN                ⎪
                            ⎪ >                           ⎪
START file-name [KEY IS ⎨ NOT LESS THAN              ⎬ data-name]
                            ⎪ NOT <                       ⎪
                            ⎪ GREATER THAN OR EQUAL TO    ⎪
                            ⎩ >=                          ⎭

    [INVALID KEY imperative-statement-1]
    [NOT INVALID KEY imperative-statement-2]
    [END-START]
```

Figure 4-1   COBOL elements for sequential processing of relative record files (part 1 of 2)

```
READ file-name [NEXT] RECORD
     [INTO data-name]
     [AT END imperative-statement-1]
     [NOT AT END imperative-statement-2]
     [END-READ]


WRITE record-name
     [FROM data-name]
     [INVALID KEY imperative-statement-1]
     [NOT INVALID KEY imperative-statement-2]
     [END-WRITE]


REWRITE record-name
     [FROM data-name]
     [INVALID KEY imperative-statement-1]
     [NOT INVALID KEY imperative-statement-2]
     [END-REWRITE]


DELETE file-name RECORD
     [END-DELETE]


CLOSE file-name ...
```

Note: The new features for VS COBOL II are shaded.

Figure 4-1   COBOL elements for sequential processing of relative record files (part 2 of 2)

processing an RRDS sequentially, the READ statement skips any empty record slots in the file. If, for example, you're sequentially reading an RRDS that doesn't have a record in slot 6, after the record in slot 5 is read, the next READ statement will read the record in slot 7. So you don't have to worry about those empty record slots in your programs.

A sequential update program   Sequential processing of relative record data sets is similar to the sequential processing of key-sequenced data sets, so you shouldn't have any problems with it. In fact, the sequential update program that I'm about to present is almost identical to the sequential update program for a key-sequenced master file that I presented in chapter 2.

FILE STATUS code	Meaning
00	Sucessful completion of I/O operation
10	End of file reached during read operation (AT END condition)
14	For a read operation, the size of the relative record number is larger than the size of the relative key field for the file
22	Invalid key condition: duplicate key
23	Invalid key condition: record not found

Figure 4-2   FILE STATUS codes for I/O operations on relative record files

Figure 4-3 presents a program overview for the sequential update program. In this program, the records in an inventory master file are updated based on the data in a file of valid inventory transactions. After all the transactions for an item have been processed, the master record is rewritten to the file.

If you look at the structure chart for this program in figure 4-4, you'll see it's the same as the structure chart for the sequential update program for the key-sequenced file presented in chapter 2 (figure 2-13). If you look at the source code for this program in figure 4-5, you can see that it's nearly the same as the code in figure 2-14.

There are two things in this program that I'd like you to notice. First, the SELECT statement for the inventory master file specifies ORGANIZATION IS RELATIVE and ACCESS IS SEQUENTIAL. In this case, I didn't code the RELATIVE KEY clause since the program is going to access the file sequentially starting with the first record.

Second, although the READ statement in module 330 is coded just as you would code any sequential READ statement, it doesn't work quite the same. When you process an RRDS sequentially, the READ statement reads the records in sequence by relative record number. If a record slot is empty, it is skipped. So each READ statement in this program will read one inventory master record until there are no more records in the file.

Program: INV3100 Update inventory file (sequential)	**Page:** 1
Designer: Mike Murach	**Date:** 9-03-86

Input/output specifications

File	Description	Use
VALTRAN	Valid inventory transaction file	Input
INVMAST	Inventory master file	Update
ERRTRAN	Unmatched inventory transaction file	Output

Process specifications

This program updates an inventory master file (INVMAST) based on the data in a file of valid inventory transaction records (VALTRAN). The program reads the master file on a sequential basis and rewrites the updated records to the master file.

To compute the relative record number for a master record, you subtract 10,000 from the record's item number. As a result, the records in the master file are in sequence by item number. That's why they can be updated on a sequential basis. VALTRAN is also in item number sequence.

If a transaction has the same item number as a master record, the transaction matches the master record. Then, the transaction data is used to update the master record. The on hand quantity in the master record increases by the receipt quantity in the transaction record.

If a matching master record can't be found for a transaction, the transaction is unmatched. Then, the program writes the transaction record on the file of error transactions (ERRTRAN). The record formats for VALTRAN and ERRTRAN are the same.

The basic processing requirements are:

1. Read a transaction record.

2. If necessary, get inventory master records until a record with a matching or greater item number is found. This step includes rewriting the last master record that was updated.

3. If the transaction is matched, update the matching master record.

4. If the transaction is unmatched, write the record on the file of error transactions.

Figure 4-3   The program overview for a program that sequentially updates a relative file

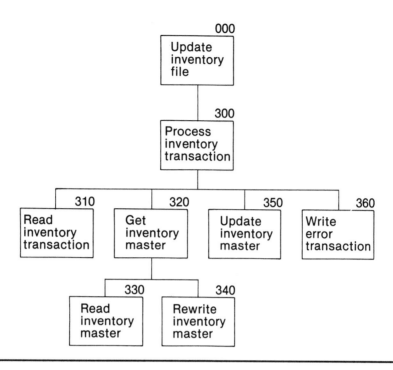

Figure 4-4   The structure chart for the sequential update program

Random processing

When you randomly process a relative record file, you use relative record numbers to locate specific records in much the same way that you use record keys when you randomly process a key-sequenced file. The main difference between a KSDS and an RRDS is that there's no index component for a relative record file. Instead, you access the data component directly. That makes random processing of an RRDS more efficient than the processing of a KSDS.

Figure 4-6 illustrates the COBOL elements you use to process a relative record data set randomly. Since the elements are so similar to the elements used for key-sequenced data sets, I'll only mention the SELECT statement.

The SELECT statement   In the SELECT statement, you specify ORGANIZATION IS RELATIVE and ACCESS IS RANDOM. In addition, you have to include the RELATIVE KEY clause. You must define this field as an unsigned numeric field in the Working-Storage Section. You can't define this field in the record description in the File Section.

```
 IDENTIFICATION DIVISION.
*
 PROGRAM-ID.  INV3100.
*
 ENVIRONMENT DIVISION.
*
 INPUT-OUTPUT SECTION.
*
 FILE-CONTROL.
     SELECT VALTRAN  ASSIGN TO SYS020-AS-VALTRAN.
     SELECT INVMAST  ASSIGN TO SYS021-INVMAST
                     ORGANIZATION IS RELATIVE
                     ACCESS IS SEQUENTIAL
                     FILE STATUS IS INVMAST-ERROR-CODE.
     SELECT ERRTRAN  ASSIGN TO SYS022-AS-ERRTRAN
                     ORGANIZATION IS SEQUENTIAL
                     ACCESS IS SEQUENTIAL
                     FILE STATUS IS ERRTRAN-ERROR-CODE.
*
 DATA DIVISION.
*
 FILE SECTION.
*
 FD  VALTRAN
     LABEL RECORDS ARE STANDARD
     RECORD CONTAINS 21 CHARACTERS.
*
 01  VALID-TRANSACTION-AREA      PIC X(21).
*
 FD  INVMAST
     LABEL RECORDS ARE STANDARD
     RECORD CONTAINS 50 CHARACTERS.
*
 01  MASTER-RECORD-AREA          PIC X(50).
*
 FD  ERRTRAN
     LABEL RECORDS ARE STANDARD
     RECORD CONTAINS 21 CHARACTERS.
*
 01  ERROR-TRANSACTION           PIC X(21).
*
 WORKING-STORAGE SECTION.
*
```

Figure 4-5   The sequential update program (part 1 of 4)

```
01  SWITCHES.
*
    05  ALL-RECORDS-PROCESSED-SWITCH     PIC X    VALUE 'N'.
        88  ALL-RECORDS-PROCESSED                 VALUE 'Y'.
    05  MASTER-UPDATED-SWITCH            PIC X    VALUE 'N'.
        88  MASTER-UPDATED                        VALUE 'Y'.
*
01  FILE-STATUS-FIELDS.
*
    05  INVMAST-ERROR-CODE      PIC XX.
    05  ERRTRAN-ERROR-CODE      PIC XX.
*
01  INVENTORY-TRANSACTION.
*
    05  IT-ITEM-NO              PIC X(5).
    05  IT-VENDOR-NO            PIC X(5).
    05  IT-RECEIPT-DATE         PIC X(6).
    05  IT-RECEIPT-QUANTITY     PIC S9(5).
*
01  INVENTORY-MASTER-RECORD.
*
    05  IM-DESCRIPTIVE-DATA.
        10  IM-ITEM-NO          PIC X(5).
        10  IM-ITEM-DESC        PIC X(20).
        10  IM-UNIT-COST        PIC S999V99.
        10  IM-UNIT-PRICE       PIC S999V99.
    05  IM-INVENTORY-DATA.
        10  IM-REORDER-POINT    PIC S9(5).
        10  IM-ON-HAND          PIC S9(5).
        10  IM-ON-ORDER         PIC S9(5).
*
 PROCEDURE DIVISION.
*
 000-UPDATE-INVENTORY-FILE.
*
    OPEN INPUT   VALTRAN
         I-O     INVMAST
         OUTPUT  ERRTRAN.
    MOVE LOW-VALUE TO IM-ITEM-NO.
    PERFORM 300-PROCESS-INVENTORY-TRAN
        UNTIL ALL-RECORDS-PROCESSED.
    CLOSE VALTRAN
          INVMAST
          ERRTRAN.
    DISPLAY 'INV3100  I  1   NORMAL EOJ'.
    STOP RUN.
*
```

Figure 4-5   The sequential update program (part 2 of 4)

```
300-PROCESS-INVENTORY-TRAN.
*
    PERFORM 310-READ-INVENTORY-TRAN.
    PERFORM 320-GET-INVENTORY-MASTER
        UNTIL IM-ITEM-NO NOT < IT-ITEM-NO.
    IF        IM-ITEM-NO = HIGH-VALUE
        AND IT-ITEM-NO = HIGH-VALUE
        MOVE 'Y' TO ALL-RECORDS-PROCESSED-SWITCH
    ELSE
        IF IM-ITEM-NO = IT-ITEM-NO
            PERFORM 350-UPDATE-INVENTORY-MASTER
        ELSE
            PERFORM 360-WRITE-ERROR-TRAN.
*
310-READ-INVENTORY-TRAN.
*
    READ VALTRAN INTO INVENTORY-TRANSACTION
        AT END
            MOVE HIGH-VALUE TO IT-ITEM-NO.
*
320-GET-INVENTORY-MASTER.
*
    IF MASTER-UPDATED
        PERFORM 340-REWRITE-INVENTORY-MASTER.
    IF NOT MASTER-UPDATED
        PERFORM 330-READ-INVENTORY-MASTER.
*
330-READ-INVENTORY-MASTER.
*
    READ INVMAST INTO INVENTORY-MASTER-RECORD.
    IF INVMAST-ERROR-CODE NOT = '00'
        MOVE HIGH-VALUE TO IM-ITEM-NO
        IF INVMAST-ERROR-CODE NOT = '10'
            DISPLAY 'INV3100   A   2   READ ERROR FOR INVMAST'
            DISPLAY 'INV3100   A   2   ITEM NUMBER = ' IM-ITEM-NO
            DISPLAY 'INV3100   A   2   FILE STATUS = '
                INVMAST-ERROR-CODE
            MOVE HIGH-VALUE TO IT-ITEM-NO.
*
```

Figure 4-5   The sequential update program (part 3 of 4)

```
340-REWRITE-INVENTORY-MASTER.
*
    REWRITE MASTER-RECORD-AREA FROM INVENTORY-MASTER-RECORD.
    IF INVMAST-ERROR-CODE NOT = '00'
        DISPLAY 'INV3100  A 3   REWRITE ERROR FOR INVMAST'
        DISPLAY 'INV3100  A 3   ITEM NUMBER = ' IM-ITEM-NO
        DISPLAY 'INV3100  A 3   FILE STATUS = '
            INVMAST-ERROR-CODE
        MOVE HIGH-VALUE TO IT-ITEM-NO
        MOVE HIGH-VALUE TO IM-ITEM-NO
    ELSE
        MOVE 'N' TO MASTER-UPDATED-SWITCH.
*
350-UPDATE-INVENTORY-MASTER.
*
    ADD IT-RECEIPT-QUANTITY TO IM-ON-HAND.
    MOVE 'Y' TO MASTER-UPDATED-SWITCH.
*
360-WRITE-ERROR-TRAN.
*
    WRITE ERROR-TRANSACTION FROM INVENTORY-TRANSACTION.
    IF ERRTRAN-ERROR-CODE NOT EQUAL '00'
        DISPLAY 'INV3100  A 4   WRITE ERROR FOR ERRTRAN'
        DISPLAY 'INV3100  A 4   ITEM NUMBER = ' IT-ITEM-NO
        DISPLAY 'INV3100  A 4   FILE STATUS = '
            ERRTRAN-ERROR-CODE
```

Figure 4-5   The sequential update program (part 4 of 4)

A random update program   Figure 4-7 presents a program overview for a program that updates an RRDS of inventory records based on the data in a sequential file of valid inventory transactions. This program is just like the sequential update program I presented earlier in this chapter, except that the records are processed on a random, rather than a sequential, basis.

As you can see in the program overview, I have assumed that the transaction file is in no particular sequence, so the program reads a transaction, reads the master record with the same item number, updates the master record, and then rewrites it. If the transaction file were in sequence by item number, however, this would be inefficient. In that case, the program should check to make sure that all the transactions for a record have been processed before the master record is rewritten to the file.

Figure 4-8 presents the structure chart for this program. It has modules to read an inventory transaction, to read a master record on a

SELECT statement

```
SELECT file-name
    ASSIGN TO system-name
    ORGANIZATION IS RELATIVE
    ACCESS MODE IS RANDOM
    RELATIVE KEY IS data-name-1
    [FILE STATUS IS data-name-2 [vsam-code]]
```

Note: Both the RELATIVE KEY field and the FILE STATUS field must be defined in working storage.

Figure 4-6   COBOL elements for random processing of relative record files (part 1 of 2)

random basis, to update the data in the master record, to rewrite the master record, and to write an error transaction. All of these modules are controlled by module 300.

Figure 4-9 presents the source code for this program. It should be easy enough to understand. Notice the SELECT statement for the relative record data set, INVMAST. Here, I specified ORGANIZATION IS RELATIVE and ACCESS IS RANDOM. I also coded the RELATIVE KEY clause since the program is going to access the file randomly. Then, I defined the relative key, INVMAST-RR-NUMBER, as an unsigned numeric field in the Working-Storage Section.

Also notice in module 320 that before the program reads a master record, it converts the item number into an RRN by subtracting 10,000 from the IT-ITEM-NO value. After that, the program issues the random READ statement.

Dynamic processing

When you access one record in a relative record file on a random basis, the next records in sequence usually don't have any relationship to it. That's why you probably won't ever want to use dynamic processing for relative record files. If you ever do need dynamic processing, though, it's much like the dynamic processing for key-sequenced files.

When you process an RRDS dynamically, you code ACCESS MODE IS DYNAMIC in the SELECT statement for the file. Then, you can use both the COBOL elements for sequential processing in figure 4-1 and the COBOL elements for random processing in figure 4-6.

When you code a sequential READ statement, remember to use the NEXT parameter. Otherwise, the compiler will assume you want to perform a random read.

FD statement

```
FD  file-name
    [LABEL RECORDS ARE STANDARD]
    [RECORD CONTAINS integer CHARACTERS]
```

Procedure Division statements

```
        INPUT   file-name-1 ...
OPEN    OUTPUT  file-name-2 ...  ...
        I-O     file-name-3 ...


READ file-name RECORD
    [INTO data-name]
    [INVALID KEY imperative-statement-1]
    [NOT INVALID KEY imperative-statement-2]
    [END-READ]


WRITE record-name
    [FROM data-name]
    [INVALID KEY imperative-statement-1]
    [NOT INVALID KEY imperative-statement-2]
    [END-WRITE]


REWRITE record-name
    [FROM data-name]
    [INVALID KEY imperative-statement-1]
    [NOT INVALID KEY imperative-statement-2]
    [END-REWRITE]


DELETE file-name RECORD
    [INVALID KEY imperative-statement-1]
    [NOT INVALID KEY imperative-statement-2]
    [END-DELETE]


CLOSE file-name ...
```

Note: The new features for VS COBOL II are shaded.

Figure 4-6   COBOL elements for random processing of relative record files (part 2 of 2)

Program: INV3200 Update inventory file (random)	Page: 1
Designer: Mike Murach	Date: 09-03-86

Input/output specifications

File	Description	Use
VALTRAN	Valid inventory transaction file	Input
INVMAST	Inventory master file	Update
ERRTRAN	Unmatched inventory transaction file	Output

Process specifications

This program updates an inventory master file (INVMAST) based on the data in a file of valid inventory transaction records (VALTRAN). It updates the file on a random basis. To calculate the record number for a master record, the program subtracts 10,000 from its item number.

If a master record is found for a transaction, the program uses the transaction data to update the master record. The on hand quantity in the master record increases by the receipt quantity in the transaction record.

If a master record is not found for a transaction, the program writes the transaction record on the file of error transactions (ERRTRAN). The record format for ERRTRAN is the same as for VALTRAN.

The basic processing requirements are:

1. Read a transaction record.

2. Read the master record with the same item number as in the transaction record.

3. If a master record is found, update the master record.

4. If the master record is not found, write the transaction record on the file of error transactions.

Figure 4-7   The program overview for a program that randomly updates a relative file

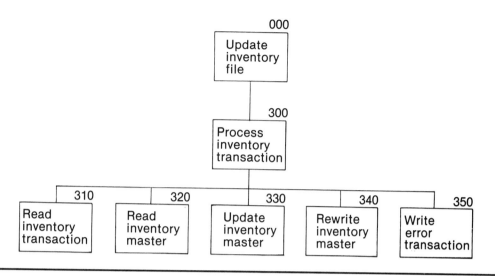

Figure 4-8   The structure chart for the random update program

Discussion

Although relative record files can be useful occasionally, you probably won't ever use them for one of three reasons. First, it's usually difficult to convert a field in a master record to a unique relative record number. Second, a relative record file is likely to use disk space inefficiently due to the number of empty record areas it contains. Third, you can't use alternate keys with a relative record data set.

Terminology

slot
relative record number
RRN

Objective

Given specifications for a program that processes a relative record data set, code a COBOL solution.

```
 IDENTIFICATION DIVISION.
*
 PROGRAM-ID.  INV3200.
*
 ENVIRONMENT DIVISION.
*
 INPUT-OUTPUT SECTION.
*
 FILE-CONTROL.
     SELECT VALTRAN  ASSIGN TO SYS020-AS-VALTRAN.
     SELECT INVMAST  ASSIGN TO SYS021-INVMAST
                     ORGANIZATION IS RELATIVE
                     ACCESS IS RANDOM
                     RELATIVE KEY IS INVMAST-RR-NUMBER
                     FILE STATUS IS INVMAST-ERROR-CODE.
     SELECT ERRTRAN  ASSIGN TO SYS022-AS-ERRTRAN
                     ORGANIZATION IS SEQUENTIAL
                     ACCESS IS SEQUENTIAL
                     FILE STATUS IS ERRTRAN-ERROR-CODE.
*
 DATA DIVISION.
*
 FILE SECTION.
*
 FD  VALTRAN
     LABEL RECORDS ARE STANDARD
     RECORD CONTAINS 21 CHARACTERS.
*
 01  VALID-TRANSACTION-AREA      PIC X(21).
*
 FD  INVMAST
     LABEL RECORDS ARE STANDARD
     RECORD CONTAINS 50 CHARACTERS.
*
 01  MASTER-RECORD-AREA          PIC X(50).
*
 FD  ERRTRAN
     LABEL RECORDS ARE STANDARD
     RECORD CONTAINS 21 CHARACTERS.
*
 01  ERROR-TRANSACTION           PIC X(21).
*
```

Figure 4-9   The random update program (part 1 of 4)

```
WORKING-STORAGE SECTION.
*
01  SWITCHES.
*
    05  VALTRAN-EOF-SWITCH        PIC X    VALUE 'N'.
        88  VALTRAN-EOF                   VALUE 'Y'.
    05  MASTER-FOUND-SWITCH      PIC X.
        88  MASTER-FOUND                  VALUE 'Y'.
*
01  FILE-STATUS-FIELDS.
*
    05  INVMAST-ERROR-CODE       PIC XX.
    05  ERRTRAN-ERROR-CODE       PIC XX.
*
01  KEY-FIELD.
*
    05  INVMAST-RR-NUMBER        PIC 9(5).
*
01  INVENTORY-TRANSACTION.
*
    05  IT-ITEM-NO               PIC 9(5).
    05  IT-VENDOR-NO             PIC X(5).
    05  IT-RECEIPT-DATE          PIC X(6).
    05  IT-RECEIPT-QUANTITY      PIC S9(5).
*
01  INVENTORY-MASTER-RECORD.
*
    05  IM-DESCRIPTIVE-DATA.
        10  IM-ITEM-NO           PIC 9(5).
        10  IM-ITEM-DESC         PIC X(20).
        10  IM-UNIT-COST         PIC S999V99.
        10  IM-UNIT-PRICE        PIC S999V99.
    05  IM-INVENTORY-DATA.
        10  IM-REORDER-POINT     PIC S9(5).
        10  IM-ON-HAND           PIC S9(5).
        10  IM-ON-ORDER          PIC S9(5).
*
PROCEDURE DIVISION.
*
000-UPDATE-INVENTORY-FILE.
*
    OPEN INPUT   VALTRAN
         I-O     INVMAST
         OUTPUT ERRTRAN.
    PERFORM 300-PROCESS-INVENTORY-TRAN
        UNTIL VALTRAN-EOF.
    CLOSE VALTRAN
          INVMAST
          ERRTRAN.
    DISPLAY 'INV3200 I 1  NORMAL EOJ'.
    STOP RUN.
```

Figure 4-9   The random update program (part 2 of 4)

```
*
 300-PROCESS-INVENTORY-TRAN.
*
     PERFORM 310-READ-INVENTORY-TRAN.
     IF NOT VALTRAN-EOF
         PERFORM 320-READ-INVENTORY-MASTER.
     IF NOT VALTRAN-EOF
         IF MASTER-FOUND
             PERFORM 330-UPDATE-INVENTORY-MASTER
             PERFORM 340-REWRITE-INVENTORY-MASTER
         ELSE
             PERFORM 350-WRITE-ERROR-TRAN.
*
 310-READ-INVENTORY-TRAN.
*
     READ VALTRAN INTO INVENTORY-TRANSACTION
         AT END
             MOVE 'Y' TO VALTRAN-EOF-SWITCH.
*
 320-READ-INVENTORY-MASTER.
*
     SUBTRACT 10000 FROM IT-ITEM-NO GIVING INVMAST-RR-NUMBER.
     MOVE 'Y' TO MASTER-FOUND-SWITCH.
     READ INVMAST INTO INVENTORY-MASTER-RECORD.
     IF INVMAST-ERROR-CODE NOT = '00'
         MOVE 'N' TO MASTER-FOUND-SWITCH
         IF INVMAST-ERROR-CODE NOT = '23'
             DISPLAY 'INV3200  A  2   READ ERROR FOR INVMAST'
             DISPLAY 'INV3200  A  2   ITEM NUMBER = ' IT-ITEM-NO
             DISPLAY 'INV3200  A  2   FILE STATUS = '
                 INVMAST-ERROR-CODE
             MOVE 'Y' TO VALTRAN-EOF-SWITCH.
*
 330-UPDATE-INVENTORY-MASTER.
*
     ADD IT-RECEIPT-QUANTITY TO IM-ON-HAND.
*
 340-REWRITE-INVENTORY-MASTER.
*
     REWRITE MASTER-RECORD-AREA FROM INVENTORY-MASTER-RECORD.
     IF INVMAST-ERROR-CODE NOT = '00'
         DISPLAY 'INV3200  A  3   REWRITE ERROR FOR INVMAST'
         DISPLAY 'INV3200  A  3   ITEM NUMBER = ' IM-ITEM-NO
         DISPLAY 'INV3200  A  3   FILE STATUS = '
             INVMAST-ERROR-CODE
         MOVE 'Y' TO VALTRAN-EOF-SWITCH.
```

Figure 4-9   The random update program (part 3 of 4)

```
*
 350-WRITE-ERROR-TRAN.
*
    WRITE ERROR-TRANSACTION FROM INVENTORY-TRANSACTION.
    IF ERRTRAN-ERROR-CODE NOT = '00'
        DISPLAY 'INV3200  A  4  WRITE ERROR FOR ERRTRAN'
        DISPLAY 'INV3200  A  4  ITEM NUMBER = ' IT-ITEM-NO
        DISPLAY 'INV3200  A  4  FILE STATUS = '
            ERRTRAN-ERROR-CODE
        MOVE 'Y' TO VALTRAN-EOF-SWITCH.
```

Figure 4-9   The random update program (part 4 of 4)

JCL and the Access Method Services program

The two chapters in this section complete the things you need to know to work with VSAM data sets. In chapter 5, you'll learn how to code the job control statements to allocate VSAM files for use in your application programs. Then, in chapter 6, you'll learn how to use the Access Method Services (IDCAMS) utility program to create, modify, and manage VSAM data sets.

Chapter 5

The JCL requirements for VSAM data sets

One of the original design objectives of VSAM was to eliminate, or at least reduce, the need for JCL statements to allocate data sets. VSAM accomplishes this JCL simplification by centralizing functions such as defining, deleting, and altering file characteristics in the AMS utility program. As a result, the JCL requirements for VSAM files are much simpler than the JCL requirements for files of other access methods.

Don't misunderstand, though. The use of VSAM doesn't eliminate complexity, it just transfers it from JCL to the AMS utility program. In chapter 6, you'll see just how complicated AMS jobs can be.

In this chapter, you'll learn how to code JCL statements for jobs that process VSAM files. Because MVS and VSE have completely different JCL requirements, the material on JCL is divided into two topics. The first topic covers MVS JCL, and the second topic covers VSE JCL. That way, you can read just the topic that applies to your system.

Keep in mind, however, that I won't teach you how to use job control language in this chapter; that's beyond the scope of this book. Instead, I'll show you the format of the JCL statements that are unique to VSAM file processing. If you want to learn more about coding job control language for either MVS or VSE systems, I recommend that you read one of our JCL books: *MVS JCL* or *DOS/VSE JCL*. They'll teach you the JCL you need to know to process both VSAM and non-VSAM files.

Topic 1 MVS JCL for VSAM data sets

To code the MVS JCL for jobs that process VSAM files, you need to know two things: how to code DD statements for VSAM files and how MVS searches its catalogs to find a file you specify.

The DD statement for VSAM files

Figure 5-1 shows the format of the DD statement for VSAM files. The syntax of the DD statement is identical for all three types of VSAM files. As you can see, I've included just three parameters in figure 5-1: DSNAME, DUMMY, and DISP. As I describe these parameters, you can refer to the DD statement examples in figure 5-2.

The DSNAME parameter   As you can see in figure 5-1, the DSNAME parameter supplies the name of the VSAM data set. The name you specify in the DSNAME parameter is the name that was given to the data set when it was defined in AMS.

The DUMMY parameter   The DUMMY parameter lets you simulate a VSAM file without actually processing a file. When a program tries to read data from a DUMMY file, VSAM returns an end of file indication. And when a program tries to write data to the file, the data is simply discarded.

When you process a dummy VSAM file, you must also specify AMP=AMORG, indicating that the file being accessed is a VSAM file. Normally, MVS realizes that a VSAM file is being processed when it retrieves the catalog information for the file. But when you specify DUMMY, MVS doesn't search the catalog, so you need the AMP parameter.

The DISP parameter   For a VSAM file, the DISP parameter has just one function: it indicates whether or not the file can be processed simultaneously by more than one job. If you specify DISP=SHR, as in example 1 in figure 5-2, the file can be shared by several jobs running at the same time. If you specify DISP=OLD, as in example 2, the file can not be shared; the job processing it has exclusive access to it. The type of sharing allowed when you specify DISP=SHR depends on how you code the SHAREOPTIONS parameter when you define the file under AMS. You'll learn how to do that in the next chapter.

```
//ddname    DD    DSNAME=data-set-name    ,DISP=    SHR
                  DUMMY,AMP=AMORG                    OLD
```

Parameter	Explanation
ddname	Specifies the one- to eight-character name used by the application program to identify the file.
DSNAME	Specifies the name of the VSAM data set. The name you code must be the same as the one specified when the file was defined. Normally, the high-level qualifier of the name identifies the owning catalog.
DUMMY	Specifies that a VSAM file should not be allocated; instead, MVS should simulate a VSAM file.
DISP	Specifies the status of the data set. Code OLD for exclusive access, SHR for shared access.

Figure 5-1   The DD statement for VSAM files

The DD statement for alternate indexes

You need to code a DD statement for each alternate index path you specify in your program. To form the ddname for each path, use the assignment name for the file followed by a number: 1 for the first alternate index you specify in the SELECT statement, 2 for the second, and so on. If the resulting name is longer than eight characters, drop characters from the end of the file's assignment name. For example, if the assignment name for a data set is CUSTMAST, the ddnames for the first two alternate indexes you specify would be CUSTMAS1 and CUSTMAS2. Example 4 in figure 5-2 illustrates DD statements for a file named EMPMAST and two of its alternate indexes.

Catalog considerations

As I explained in chapter 1, all VSAM files must be cataloged in a user catalog or in the master catalog. Under MVS, the first group of characters in a data set name (known as the *high-level qualifier*) indicates the user catalog that owns the file. For example, a file with the name MMA2.INVENTORY.MASTER is cataloged in the user catalog called MMA2. Since the file name indicates the user catalog, no special coding is required to identify it.

But the high-level qualifier and the user catalog name are not always the same. As a matter of fact, it's more common for the high-level qualifier to be an *alias* of the actual name. (An alias is simply an alternate name for a user catalog.) By using aliases, you can catalog

Example 1: Allocating a VSAM file for shared access

```
//CUSTMAST   DD     DSNAME=MMA2.CUSTOMER.MASTER,DISP=SHR
```

Example 2: Allocating a VSAM file for exclusive access

```
//CUSTMAST   DD     DSNAME=MMA2.CUSTOMER.MASTER,DISP=OLD
```

Example 3: Allocating a dummy VSAM file

```
//PAYTRAN    DD     DUMMY,AMP=AMORG
```

Example 4: Allocating a VSAM file and two alternate indexes for shared access

```
//EMPMAST    DD     DSNAME=ACCT.EMPLOYEE.MASTER,DISP=SHR,
//EMPMAST1   DD     DSNAME=ACCT.EMPMAST.SSNUMBER.PATH,DISP=SHR
//EMPMAST2   DD     DSNAME=ACCT.EMPMAST.LAST.NAME.PATH,DISP=SHR
```

Figure 5-2   Examples of DD statements for VSAM files

files with different high-level qualifiers in the same user catalog. For example, suppose MMA2 and DEPT5 are both aliases for a user catalog named VCAT.MPS800. Then, any files with a high-level qualifier of either MMA2 or DEPT5 are cataloged in VCAT.MPS800.

Although it's uncommon, you may need to override the user catalog indicated by the high-level qualifier. You can do this by coding a JOBCAT DD statement before the first job step to identify a *job catalog* to be used throughout the job to locate data sets. Or, within a job step, you can code a STEPCAT DD statement to identify a *step catalog* to be used for a single job step. If you code a JOBCAT DD statement, MVS searches the job catalog for each data set in the job before it uses the high-level qualifier. And if you specify a STEPCAT DD statement within a job step, MVS searches the step catalog before it searches the job catalog or uses the high-level qualifier.

For example, suppose you code this statement at the beginning of a job:

```
//JOBCAT   DD    DSNAME=ACCT.USER.CATALOG,DISP=SHR
```

Then, MVS searches the user catalog named ACCT.USER.CATALOG to locate the data sets required by the job. If MVS can't find one of the files in the job catalog, it looks in the user catalog indicated by the file's high-level qualifier. If MVS still can't find the file, it looks in the master

```
//DLOWE2A    JOB     USER=DLOWE2,PASSWORD=XXXXXXXX
//INV1200    EXEC    PGM=INV1200
//VALTRAN    DD      DSNAME=MMA.VALID.TRANS.FILE,DISP=SHR
//INVMAST    DD      DSNAME=MMA.INVEN.MASTER.FILE,DISP=SHR
//ERRTRAN    DD      DSNAME=MMA.ERROR.TRANS.FILE,DISP=SHR
```

Figure 5-3   An MVS job stream to run the random update program presented in figure 2-18

catalog. (Under normal circumstances, you shouldn't define files in the master catalog.)

If your job or job step uses data sets from more than one user catalog, you must link the catalogs together in the JOBCAT or STEPCAT DD statement, like this:

```
//JOBCAT    DD    DSNAME=ACCT.USER.CATALOG,DISP=SHR
//          DD    DSNAME=GROUP2.USER.CATALOG,DISP=SHR
```

Here, MVS will search the two user catalogs ACCT.USER.CATALOG and GROUP2.USER.CATALOG, in that order, to locate the VSAM files used by the job.

You probably won't use either JOBCAT or STEPCAT very often. In fact, you may never use them at all. Instead, you'll use the high-level qualifier to indicate the user catalog that owns the files you want to use. To give you an idea of how your JCL will usually look, figure 5-3 contains the JCL you would need to run the random update program presented in figure 2-18.

Discussion

With this background, you should be able to code JCL statements for jobs that use VSAM files. Because most of a VSAM file's specifications are stored in its catalog, the DD statements for VSAM files are relatively simple.

Terminology

high-level qualifier   job catalog
alias   step catalog

Objectives

Code a DD statement to identify a VSAM file.

Topic 2   DOS/VSE JCL for VSAM data sets

To process VSAM files under VSE, you need to know how to code four things: a DLBL statement to identify a VSAM file, a DLBL statement to identify a VSAM catalog, a DLBL statement to identify an alternate index, and an EXEC statement to invoke a program that processes VSAM files.

The DLBL statement for VSAM files

Figure 5-4 shows the format of the DLBL statement for VSAM files. As I describe how to use this statement, you can refer to the DLBL statement examples in figure 5-5.

In the DLBL statement, you code the name your application program uses for the VSAM file in the file-name field. In the file-id field, you code the name that was given to the file when it was defined in AMS. And you always code VSAM to indicate that the file is a VSAM file.

The CAT operand   The CAT operand simply names the catalog that owns the file. Most of the time, though, you won't have to code this operand. (You'll see why in a moment.) The examples in figure 5-5 show DLBL statements with and without the CAT operand.

The DLBL statement for VSAM catalogs

All jobs that access VSAM files require a DLBL statement for the VSAM master catalog. The file-name of the master catalog is *IJSYSCT*, and its DLBL statement should look like example 3 in figure 5-5. Because it's a universal requirement for jobs that access VSAM files, this DLBL statement should be stored as a system standard label. If it isn't, have your systems programmer add the proper DLBL statement to the system start-up job stream that loads the label information area.

In addition to identifying the master catalog, you also have to identify the user catalogs that own the VSAM files your job will process. The usual way to specify a user catalog is to define a *job catalog* in your job stream. A job catalog is a VSAM user catalog that owns most, or all, of the files your job uses. To specify a job catalog, you code a DLBL statement with the file-name *IJSYSUC*, as in example 4 in figure 5-5. Here, the job catalog is AR.USER.CATALOG. If you code a DLBL statement like the one in this example, the system assumes that all of the VSAM files you want to access are owned by the job catalog rather than the

```
// DLBL    file-name,'file-id',,VSAM[,CAT=catalog-name]
```

Parameter	Explanation
file-name	Specifies the three- to seven-character name used by the application program to identify the file.
file-id	Specifies the name of the VSAM data set. The name you code must be the same as the one specified when the file was defined.
VSAM	Specifies that the file is a VSAM file.
CAT	Specifies the file-name on the DLBL statement that identifies the catalog that owns the file.

Figure 5-4   The DLBL statement for VSAM files

master catalog. Since most applications are designed so related files are owned by the same user catalog, this works well. Notice that I coded CAT=IJSYSCT in this example to indicate that the master catalog owns AR.USER.CATALOG.

To access a file that isn't owned by the job catalog, you can code the CAT operand in its DLBL statement. For that to work, you need to code a DLBL statement for the other user catalog with a name other than IJSYSUC. Then, the file-name from the DLBL statement for the other catalog must agree with the name you code in the file's DLBL CAT operand.

To illustrate, suppose a program named AR9000 uses four VSAM files it calls CUSTMAS, OPNITEM, PDBILL, and BADDEBT. Their VSAM names are CUSTOMER.MASTER.FILE, AR.OPEN.ITEMS, AR.PAID.BILLS, and AR.BAD.DEBTS. All files are owned by AR.USER.CATALOG, except CUSTMAS; it's owned by MMA.USER.CATALOG. Figure 5-6 shows how you can identify these files. It includes DLBL statements for the two user catalogs the application requires. I used AR.USER.CATALOG as the job catalog because it owns three of the four files AR9000 uses. As a result, I didn't have to code the CAT operand in the DLBL statements for those three files. However, I did have to code the CAT operand in the DLBL statement for the fourth file, CUSTMAS. The name I coded in the CAT operand is MMACAT, the file-name in the DLBL statement for the catalog that owns it.

Example 1 Allocating a VSAM file in the current job catalog

```
// DLBL     INVMAST,'INVENTORY.MASTER.FILE',,VSAM
```

Example 2 Allocating a VSAM file that's not in the current job catalog

```
// DLBL     ARCAT,'AR.USER.CATALOG',,VSAM,CAT=IJSYSCT
// DLBL     ERRTRAN,'ERROR.TRANSACTION.FILE',,VSAM,CAT=ARCAT
```

Example 3 Allocating the VSAM master catalog

```
// DLBL     IJSYSCT,'VSAM.MASTER.CATALOG',,VSAM
```

Example 4 Allocating a VSAM job catalog

```
// DLBL     IJSYSUC,'AR.USER.CATALOG',,VSAM,CAT=IJSYSCT
```

Example 5 Allocating a VSAM file and two alternate indexes

```
// DLBL     EMPMAST,'EMPLOYEE.MASTER.FILE',,VSAM
// DLBL     EMPMAS1,'EMPMAST.SSNUMBER.PATH',,VSAM
// DLBL     EMPMAS2,'EMPMAST.LAST.NAME.PATH',,VSAM
```

Figure 5-5   Examples of DLBL statements for VSAM files and catalogs

The DLBL statement for alternate indexes

You need to code a DLBL statement for every alternate index path you
specify in the SELECT statement in your COBOL program. To form the
file-name for each path, use the system name for the file followed by a
number: 1 for the first alternate index you specify in the SELECT statement, 2 for the second, and so on. If the resulting name is longer than
seven characters, drop characters from the end of the file's assignment
name. So if the assignment name for a data set was CUSTMST and the
program used two alternate indexes for that data set, the file-names for
the two alternate indexes would be CUSTMS1 and CUSTMS2. Example
5 in figure 5-5 shows the DLBL statements for a file named EMPMAST
and its two alternate indexes.

The EXEC statement for programs that access VSAM files

When you invoke a program that uses VSAM, you must insure that
there's enough available storage for VSAM to allocate its I/O buffers and

```
//  JOB      AR9000
//  DLBL     IJSYSUC,'AR.USER.CATALOG',,VSAM,CAT=IJSYSCT
//  DLBL     OPNITEM,'AR.OPEN.ITEMS',,VSAM
//  DLBL     PDBILL,'AR.PAID.BILLS',,VSAM
//  DLBL     BADDEBT,'AR.BAD.DEBTS',,VSAM
//  DLBL     MMACAT,'MMA.USER.CATALOG',,VSAM,CAT=IJSYSCT
//  DLBL     CUSTMAS,'CUSTOMER.MASTER.FILE',,VSAM,CAT=MMACAT
//  EXEC     AR9000,SIZE=AUTO
/*
/&
```

Figure 5-6   A VSE job stream to run a program that uses four VSAM files from two different catalogs

control blocks. This storage can be significant: 40K for a catalog, 12K for each KSDS, and 10K for each RRDS or ESDS.

Fortunately, you don't have to calculate VSAM's storage requirements for each program you write. Instead, just specify SIZE=AUTO in the EXEC statement, as illustrated in figure 5-6, for each program that processes VSAM files. That way, VSE will allocate as much storage as necessary.

Discussion

With this background, you should be able to code JCL statements for DOS/VSE jobs that use VSAM files. Because most of a VSAM file's specifications are stored in its catalog, the DLBL statements for VSAM files are relatively simple.

Terminology

IJSYSCT
job catalog
IJSYSUC

Objectives

1. Code a DLBL statement to identify a VSAM file, a VSAM catalog, or a VSAM alternate index.

2. Code an EXEC statement to invoke a program that processes a VSAM file.

Chapter 6

The Access Method Services program

This chapter introduces you to the Access Method Services program, or IDCAMS. Since IDCAMS is a complicated program with many more functions than you'll need to use for program development, I'll present just a subset of the available commands in this chapter. These commands will let you perform the IDCAMS functions you normally need as you develop COBOL programs. Later, if you require a more thorough understanding of IDCAMS and its commands, I recommend our complete VSAM book, *VSAM: Access Method Services and Application Programming.*

There are five topics in this chapter. In the first topic, I'll show you how to invoke IDCAMS and code its commands. In topic 2, I'll show you how to define a data set. In topic 3, I'll show you the commands for defining an alternate index and path and for building an alternate index. Then, topic 4 shows you how to use the catalog maintenance functions, and topic 5 shows you how to copy and print data sets.

Topic 1   An introduction to Access Method Services

As I told you in chapter 1, Access Method Services is a general-purpose utility program that provides a variety of services for VSAM files. This topic introduces AMS and a subset of the available AMS commands. Here, you'll learn the details of coding AMS commands, including how to code parameters and subparameters, continuation lines, and comments. Then, you'll learn how to invoke AMS from five different environments.

AMS commands

Figure 6-1 is an overview of the AMS commands this book covers. In the next four topics, I'll cover these commands in detail. Although there are other AMS commands besides those listed in figure 6-1, I don't cover them in this book because they provide functions you aren't likely to require for COBOL programming.

How to code AMS commands

You can code AMS commands anywhere in columns 2 through 72. It's easy to start your commands in column 1, however, so be sure to avoid that common mistake.

   Each AMS command follows this general format:

```
verb    parameters
```

Here, the *verb* is one of the commands listed in figure 6-1 (DEFINE CLUSTER, LISTCAT, and so on). Then, the *parameters* supply additional information that tells AMS what you want it to do. Figure 6-2 shows five examples of valid ways to code parameters in AMS commands.

Parameters and continuation lines   As you can see in figure 6-2, most commands allow you to code more than one parameter. To make the parameters easy to read, I code one parameter per line. When you do that, AMS requires that you use hyphens to continue a command from one line to the next. If you omit the hyphens, AMS will reject your command. In examples 1 and 2, I placed the hyphens after one blank following the end of each parameter. In examples 3 and 4, though, I aligned all the hyphens. The way you code the hyphens in your

AMS command	Function
ALTER	Change the information specified for a catalog, cluster, alternate index, or path at define time.
BLDINDEX	Build an alternate index.
DEFINE ALTERNATEINDEX	Define an alternate index.
DEFINE CLUSTER	Define a VSAM file, whether it's key-sequenced, entry-sequenced, or relative record.
DEFINE PATH	Define the path that relates an alternate index to its base cluster.
DELETE	Remove a catalog entry for a catalog, cluster, alternate index, or path.
LISTCAT	List information about data sets.
PRINT	Print the contents of a VSAM or non-VSAM file.
REPRO	Copy records from one file to another. The input and output files can be VSAM or non-VSAM.

Figure 6-1   AMS commands described in this chapter

commands is a matter of personal preference. Just be sure there's at least one blank between the end of the parameter and the hyphen.

Most AMS command parameters have one or more abbreviated forms. For example, you can abbreviate RECORDS as REC. And you can code CISZ or CNVSZ instead of CONTROLINTERVALSIZE. Since most of the abbreviations are harder to remember than the full form of the parameter, I use abbreviations only for long parameters like CONTROLINTERVALSIZE. As I present each parameter for a command, I'll tell you if it has any useful abbreviations.

Parameter values and subparameter lists   Most parameters require that you code a value enclosed in parentheses, like this:

```
RECORDS(500)
```

If a parameter requires more than one value, you code a *subparameter list* by separating each value with a space or a comma, like this:

```
KEYS(5 0)
```

or this:

```
ENTRIES(FILE1,FILE2,FILE3,FILE4)
```

In the examples in this book, I separate parameters and subparameters with spaces.

Parameter groups and parentheses   AMS uses parentheses to delimit groups of parameters within a command. To illustrate, consider example 2 in figure 6-2. Here, I grouped the first four parameters (NAME, INDEXED, RECORDSIZE, and KEYS) together within parentheses. That's a requirement of the DEFINE CLUSTER command. If you omit the parentheses, AMS will reject the command. After the first group of parameters, you can code two other groups in a DEFINE CLUSTER command, labeled DATA and INDEX. In example 2, I coded both of them, and I enclosed their parameters within parentheses. Notice that each parameter group ends with two adjacent right parentheses. The first marks the end of the last parameter in the group, and the second marks the end of the parameter group itself.

The syntax for using parentheses in AMS commands is confusing and will probably be the cause of most of your coding errors. To simplify things, some programmers use separate lines for the parentheses that begin and end each group of parameters, as in example 4 of figure 6-2. If that helps you reduce coding errors, by all means do it. For me, it just confuses things even more.

Comments   Example 4 in figure 6-2 illustrates how you can use *comments* along with AMS commands. A comment begins with the characters /* and ends with */. Example 4 contains two comments. One is on its own line, before the DEFINE command. The second is within the command, following the KEYS parameter. Notice that the continuation character comes after the comment.

How to invoke AMS

Now that you know how to code AMS commands, you're ready to learn how to code the necessary job control statements or commands to invoke AMS in your operating environment. Figure 6-3 shows how to invoke AMS from five different environments.

MVS JCL to invoke AMS   The first example in figure 6-3 shows how you code an AMS job on an MVS system. In it, I specified IDCAMS as the program-name in an EXEC statement. Then, I coded two DD statements: SYSPRINT and SYSIN. SYSPRINT directs the printed AMS output, and SYSIN identifies the file that contains the input commands for AMS. When you code AMS commands in the job stream, code an asterisk instead of a file name on the SYSIN DD statement, and be sure you follow the commands with an end of data statement (/*). If the

Example 1

```
LISTCAT ENTRIES(CUSTOMER.MASTER.FILE) -
        ALL
```

Example 2

```
DEFINE CLUSTER ( NAME(AR.TRANS) -
                 INDEXED -
                 RECORDSIZE(150 200) -
                 KEYS(12 0) ) -
       DATA    ( NAME(AR.TRANS.DATA) -
                 VOLUMES(VOL261 VOL262) -
                 CYLINDERS(50 50) ) -
       INDEX   ( NAME(AR.TRANS.INDEX) -
                 VOLUMES(VOL271) )
```

Example 3

```
DEFINE CLUSTER ( NAME(AR.TRANS)                    -
                 INDEXED                           -
                 RECORDSIZE(150 200)               -
                 KEYS(12 0) )                      -
       DATA    ( NAME(AR.TRANS.DATA)               -
                 VOLUMES(VOL261 VOL262)            -
                 CYLINDERS(50 50) )                -
       INDEX   ( NAME(AR.TRANS.INDEX)              -
                 VOLUMES(VOL271) )
```

Example 4

```
/* ACCOUNTS RECEIVABLE TRANSACTION FILE */
DEFINE CLUSTER (                                   -
                 NAME(AR.TRANS)                    -
                 INDEXED                           -
                 RECORDSIZE(150 200)               -
                 KEYS(12 0)  /* ACCOUNT NO */      -
               )                                   -
       DATA    (                                   -
                 NAME(AR.TRANS.DATA)               -
                 VOLUMES(VOL261 VOL262)            -
                 CYLINDERS(50 50)                  -
               )                                   -
       INDEX   (                                   -
                 NAME(AR.TRANS.INDEX)              -
                 VOLUMES(VOL271)                   -
               )
```

Example 5

```
PRINT CUSTOMER.MASTER.FILE
```

Figure 6-2   Examples of valid AMS commands

Example 1: MVS

```
//LISTCAT  JOB  ...
//         EXEC  PGM=IDCAMS
//SYSPRINT DD   SYSOUT=A
//SYSIN    DD   *
  LISTCAT ENTRIES(AR.OPEN.ITEMS)    -
          VOLUME
/*
//
```

Example 2: TSO

```
READY
listcat entries(ar.open.items) volume
.
.
```

Example 3: VSE

```
// JOB     LISTCAT
// EXEC    IDCAMS,SIZE=AUTO
   LISTCAT ENTRIES(AR.OPEN.ITEMS)    -
           CATALOG(AR.USER.CATALOG)  -
           VOLUME
/*
/&
```

Example 4: ICCF

```
/LOAD IDCAMS
/OPTION GETVIS=AUTO
 LISTCAT ENTRIES(AR.OPEN.ITEMS)    -
         CATALOG(AR.USER.CATALOG)  -
         VOLUME
```

Example 5: VM/CMS

```
CP:
edit listcat amserv
NEW FILE:
EDIT:
input
   listcat entries(ar.open.items)    -
           catalog(ar.user.catalog)  -
           volume
file
CP:
amserv listcat (print
.
.
```

Figure 6-3   Invoking AMS under MVS, TSO, VSE, ICCF, and VM/CMS

commands require that AMS process a VSAM data set, you may have to provide a DD statement for that file too.

AMS under TSO   Example 2 in figure 6-3 shows how you can invoke AMS from a TSO terminal. Here, the lower-case text represents data entered by the terminal operator and the upper-case text is a TSO message. In other words, you don't need to enter any specific command to invoke AMS under TSO. Since TSO recognizes AMS commands, it automatically invokes AMS to process them. Notice in this example that I combined the command parameters on a single line. Although I recommend that you code each parameter on a separate line in a batch file, that just doesn't make sense when you're working at a terminal. Also, if your AMS commands require access to a data set, you'll have to issue an ALLOCATE command for it before you issue the IDCAMS command.

VSE JCL to invoke AMS   The third example in figure 6-3 shows you how to invoke AMS under VSE. Here, you code an EXEC statement to invoke IDCAMS, followed by AMS commands. (Notice that I coded SIZE=AUTO on the EXEC statement.)   After the AMS commands, you code an end of data statement (/*). If the AMS commands you code process a data set, you may also have to provide a DLBL statement for that file.

AMS under ICCF   If you're using ICCF on a VSE system, you can invoke AMS for execution in an interactive partition. To do that, you create a member like the one in example 4 of figure 6-3. Here, I coded two job entry statements: the /LOAD statement invokes IDCAMS, and the /OPTION statement specifies GETVIS=AUTO. (That's the same as coding SIZE=AUTO on an EXEC statement in a batch job.) Then, the AMS commands follow the /OPTION statement. To invoke this job, you enter the /EXEC system command, specifying the name of the ICCF library member that contains the job.

AMS under VM/CMS   If you're using VSAM under VM/CMS, you issue an AMSERV command to invoke AMS, as in example 5 in figure 6-3. Again, the lower-case text represents data entered by the terminal operator and the upper-case text is VM/CMS messages. In the AMSERV command, you specify the name of a file that contains the commands you want AMS to process. In figure 6-3, I used the editor to create a file named LISTCAT that contains the LISTCAT command. The (PRINT option tells AMS to direct its printed output to a printer.

Discussion

Once you know how to invoke IDCAMS and code its commands, you're ready to learn what the commands are. So that's what you'll learn in the next four topics. With few exceptions, the coding for these commands is the same no matter what operating environment you're working in.

Terminology

verb
parameter
subparameter list
comment

Objectives

1. Given an AMS command with incorrect syntax, correct it.

2. Code the JCL or commands necessary to invoke AMS in your operating environment.

Topic 2   How to define a data set

As I explained in chapter 1, a *cluster* is another name for a VSAM file or data set. As a result, you use the DEFINE CLUSTER command to define a VSAM file. In this topic, you'll learn how to use this command to define a key-sequenced, entry-sequenced, or relative record data set.

In general, when you use the DEFINE CLUSTER command, you know that the catalog and space for your file has already been defined. Otherwise, you can use the DEFINE USERCATALOG and DEFINE SPACE commands to set up the catalog and space that you need for your files. In a normal programming environment, though, your catalogs and space should already be established. So I won't show you how to use these commands in this book

Figure 6-4 presents the format of the DEFINE CLUSTER command. As you can see, it consists of three groups of entries labeled CLUSTER, DATA, and INDEX. In contrast, the CATALOG parameter has only one entry.

When you code parameters at the CLUSTER level, they apply to the entire cluster. However, parameters you code at the DATA or INDEX level apply only to the cluster's data or index component. Although you can code many of the DEFINE CLUSTER command's parameters at any of the first three levels, you should code most of the parameters at the CLUSTER level. As I describe the parameters, I'll point out those you should code at the DATA and INDEX levels.

To help you understand the syntax of the DEFINE CLUSTER command, figure 6-5 shows three examples. The first example defines a key-sequenced data set. Here, I coded parameters at the CLUSTER, DATA, and INDEX levels. The second example defines an entry-sequenced data set. And the third defines a relative record data set. Because ESDSs and RRDSs don't have an index component, the second and third examples don't contain parameters at the INDEX level. As I describe the parameters of the DEFINE CLUSTER command, I'll refer to the syntax diagram in figure 6-4 and to the three examples in figure 6-5.

Parameters that identify the file

Three of the DEFINE CLUSTER parameters listed in figure 6-4 simply identify the file you're defining by supplying its name, who's responsible for it, and what catalog will own it.

```
DEFINE CLUSTER  ( NAME(entry-name)

                  [OWNER(owner-id)]

                     ⎧NONINDEXED⎫
                  [  ⎨INDEXED   ⎬  ]
                     ⎩NUMBERED  ⎭

                  [RECORDSIZE(avg max)]

                     ⎧SPANNED    ⎫
                  [  ⎨NONSPANNED ⎬  ]
                     ⎩           ⎭

                  [KEYS(length offset)]

                   VOLUMES(volser...)

                     ⎧CYLINDERS⎫
                     ⎪TRACKS   ⎪
                     ⎨BLOCKS   ⎬(primary [secondary])
                     ⎪RECORDS  ⎪
                     ⎩         ⎭

                     ⎧UNIQUE        ⎫
                  [  ⎨SUBALLOCATION ⎬  ]
                     ⎩              ⎭

                  [FREESPACE(ci ca)]

                  [IMBED]

                  [SHAREOPTIONS(option)]

                  [MODEL(entry-name)])

          [DATA  ( [NAME(entry-name)]

                   [VOLUMES(volser...)]

                     ⎧CYLINDERS⎫
                     ⎪TRACKS   ⎪
                  [  ⎨BLOCKS   ⎬(primary [secondary])]
                     ⎪RECORDS  ⎪
                     ⎩         ⎭

                   [CONTROLINTERVALSIZE(bytes)])]

          [INDEX ( [NAME(entry-name)]

                   [VOLUMES(volser...)]

                     ⎧CYLINDERS⎫
                     ⎪TRACKS   ⎪
                  [  ⎨BLOCKS   ⎬(primary [secondary])])]
                     ⎪RECORDS  ⎪
                     ⎩         ⎭

          [CATALOG (name)]
```

Figure 6-4   The DEFINE CLUSTER command (part 1 of 3)

Parameter	Explanation
NAME(entry-name)	Required. Specifies the name of the cluster or component.
OWNER(owner-id)	Optional. Specifies a one- to eight-character owner-id for the file.
INDEXED NONINDEXED NUMBERED	Optional. Specifies whether you're defining a KSDS (INDEXED), ESDS (NONINDEXED), or RRDS (NUMBERED) file. INDEXED is the default. Valid at the cluster level only.
RECORDSIZE(avg max)	Optional. Specifies the average and maximum length of the file's records. If it is omitted, VSAM assumes (4089 4089) for nonspanned records and (4086 32600) for spanned records.
SPANNED NONSPANNED	Optional. Specifies whether logical records can span control intervals. NONSPANNED is the default.
KEYS(length offset)	Optional. Specifies the length and offset value of the primary key for a KSDS.
VOLUMES(vol-ser...)	Required. Specifies one or more volumes that will contain the cluster or component.
primary	Required. Specifies how much space to initially allocate to the cluster or component, expressed in cylinders, tracks, blocks, or records.
secondary	Optional. Specifies the secondary space allocation for the cluster. Ignored for unique files under DOS/VSE.
UNIQUE SUBALLOCATION	Optional. Specifies whether the file is unique (occupies its own data space) or suballocated (shares space with other files). SUBALLOCATION is the default.
FREESPACE(ci ca)	Optional. Specifies the percentage of space in each control interval and the percentage of control intervals in each control area VSAM should reserve for insertions.

Figure 6-4   The DEFINE CLUSTER command (part 2 of 3)

Parameter	Explanation
IMBED	Optional. Moves sequence set records from the index storage area to the first track of the data storage area. Also duplicates records as many times as possible on that track.
SHAREOPTIONS(option)	Optional. The option specifies how the file may be shared. Use 1 for a file that can be processed by multiple jobs as long as no job opens the file for output. Use 2 for a file that can be processed by multiple jobs as long as only one job opens the file for output. Use 3 for a file that can be processed by multiple jobs for input or output. Also, use 3 for an indexed file that has one or more alternate indexes or for a file that is also going to be processed by CICS. Remember, though, that VSAM does nothing to insure the integrity of the file when you use 3.
MODEL(entry-name)	Optional. Specifies the name of an existing cluster on which this cluster is to be modeled.
CONTROLINTERVALSIZE(bytes)	Optional. Specifies the size of control intervals. Abbreviated as CISZ.
CATALOG(name)	Optional. Specifies the name of the catalog that will own the cluster. If you omit the CATALOG parameter, the stepcat, jobcat, high-level qualifier (MVS only), or master catalog identifies the catalog.

Figure 6-4   The DEFINE CLUSTER command (part 3 of 3)

The NAME parameter   When you code a value for the NAME parameter at the CLUSTER level, that name applies only to the cluster entry. Then, if you don't specify otherwise, VSAM creates a long and cryptic name for the data component (and the index component for a KSDS). To avoid this, I suggest you code the NAME parameter at all levels of your DEFINE CLUSTER command by adding DATA and INDEX to the cluster name, as I did in the examples in figure 6-5. Figure 6-6 gives you the rules you must follow when you form a VSAM name, and figure 6-7 shows you some invalid VSAM names with valid alternatives.

The OWNER parameter   The OWNER parameter supplies an eight-character value that states who's responsible for the file. VSAM uses the owner-id for documentation only; it doesn't affect the way VSAM processes the file. The first two examples in figure 6-5 specify DLOWE2 as the owner-id.

Example 1: Define a key-sequenced data set

```
DEFINE CLUSTER ( NAME(CUSTOMER.MASTER.FILE)          -
                 OWNER(DLOWE2)                        -
                 INDEXED                              -
                 RECORDSIZE(200 200)                  -
                 KEYS(9 12)                           -
                 VOLUMES(MPS800)                      -
                 UNIQUE                               -
                 FREESPACE(20 10)                     -
                 SHAREOPTIONS(3)                      -
                 IMBED )                              -
          DATA   ( NAME(CUSTOMER.MASTER.FILE.DATA)    -
                 CYLINDERS(50 5)                      -
                 CISZ(4096) )                         -
          INDEX  ( NAME(CUSTOMER.MASTER.FILE.INDEX) )
```

Example 2: Define an entry-sequenced data set

```
DEFINE CLUSTER ( NAME(TRAN.FILE)                      -
                 OWNER(DLOWE2)                        -
                 NONINDEXED                           -
                 RECORDSIZE(190 280)                  -
                 VOLUMES(MPS800) )                    -
          DATA   ( NAME(TRAN.FILE.DATA)               -
                 CYLINDERS(10 1)                      -
                 CISZ(4096) )                         -
          CATALOG ( ACCT.USER.CATALOG )
```

Example 3: Define a relative record data set

```
DEFINE CLUSTER ( NAME(ACCOUNT.MASTER.FILE)           -
                 NUMBERED                             -
                 RECORDSIZE(502 502)                  -
                 VOLUMES(MPS800)                      -
                 UNIQUE )                             -
          DATA   ( NAME(ACCOUNT.MASTER.FILE.DATA)     -
                 CYLINDERS(10 1)                      -
                 CISZ(4096) )
```

Figure 6-5   Examples of the DEFINE CLUSTER command

The CATALOG parameter   When you use the CATALOG parameter, you'll always code it as the last parameter on the DEFINE
CLUSTER command. Under MVS, if you omit this parameter, VSAM
uses the high-level qualifier of the name in the NAME parameter.

Length	1 to 44 characters (standard)
Characters	The 26 letters (A-Z) The 10 digits (0-9) The 3 national characters (@, #, and $) The hyphen (-)
Qualifiers	Data set names with more than 8 characters must be broken into qualifiers that each contain between 1 and 8 characters. Separate qualifiers from one another with periods. The periods are counted in the overall length of the data set name.
First character	The first character of each qualifier must be a letter or a national character.
Last character	The last character of a data set name should not be a period.

Figure 6-6   Rules for forming data set names

Under VSE, if you omit the CATALOG parameter, VSAM uses the job catalog. For all operating systems, VSAM uses the master catalog if it can't identify a user catalog. Only the second example in figure 6-5 uses the CATALOG parameter. In this case, VSAM will catalog the cluster in the user catalog ACCT.USER.CATALOG.

Parameters that describe the file's characteristics

The next group of DEFINE CLUSTER parameters describes the characteristics of the file: its organization, record size, and so on.

The file-type parameter   As the examples in figure 6-5 show, you code INDEXED to define a KSDS, NONINDEXED to define an ESDS, and NUMBERED to define an RRDS. If you omit this parameter, AMS defaults to INDEXED.

The RECORDSIZE parameter   The RECORDSIZE parameter specifies the length of the logical records in your file. In it, you code two values: the average record length and the maximum record length. Whether or not you code the same or different values for average and maximum record size, the file can contain records that vary in length up to the maximum you specify. When you define a relative record file, however, you should code the same value for the average and maximum length.

Invalid data set names	Valid data set names
ACCOUNTS.RECEIVABLE.FILE	ACCOUNTS.RECEIVBL.FILE
AR.TRANS.1984	AR.TRANS.Y1984
	AR.TRANS84
AR.TRANS.APR+MAY.Y84	AR.TRANS.APR.MAY.Y84
	AR.TRANS.APR84.MAY84
INVMAST.	INVMAST

Figure 6-7   Invalid data set names with valid alternatives

The SPANNED parameter   If your file will contain records that are longer than one control interval, you need to code the SPANNED parameter. Otherwise, you can let the parameter default to NONSPANNED. Usually, you'll specify 4096 for a file's control interval size, so code SPANNED only if your records are longer than that. You'll learn more about control interval sizes in a moment.

The KEYS parameter   You code the KEYS parameter at the CLUSTER or DATA level to identify a key-sequenced data set's primary key. In the KEYS parameter, you specify the length and offset value of the key. For example, to define a primary key that occupies bytes 13 through 21 in each record, you would code:

```
KEYS(9 12)
```

as I did in example 1 in figure 6-5. Since an offset starts with zero, the thirteenth byte of a record has an offset of 12.

Parameters that specify the file's space allocation

The next group of parameters specifies how VSAM allocates space to the file and how it reserves space within the file.

The VOLUMES parameter   When you code the VOLUMES parameter at the CLUSTER level, you name the disk volume or volumes the cluster will be stored on. In each of the examples in figure 6-5, the file resides on a single disk volume named MPS800.

If you code more than one volume name in the VOLUMES parameter, your file can use the additional volumes if it requires more space than what is available on a single volume. Normally, though, you'll code just one *volume serial number*, or *vol-ser*, in the VOLUMES parameter.

The UNIQUE/SUBALLOCATION parameter   You can specify whether the file should be suballocated out of existing VSAM space or created in its own space by coding the UNIQUE/SUBALLOCATION parameter. If you specify SUBALLOCATION (or let it default as in example 2 of figure 6-5), AMS suballocates the file out of VSAM space. If you specify UNIQUE, VSAM takes the space for your cluster from the non-VSAM space that's available on the volume. So whichever parameter you code, make sure there is enough space on the volume for your file.

If the file will be owned by an ICF catalog (MVS systems only), you can omit this parameter. As you learned in chapter 1, ICF catalogs do away with the concept of VSAM space. So VSAM ignores the UNIQUE/SUBALLOCATION parameter for ICF-owned files.

The space allocation parameter   You'll use the space allocation parameter to specify how much disk storage space to allocate to your file. In example 1 of figure 6-5, I coded the allocation parameter like this:

```
CYLINDERS(50 5)
```

Here, the initial space allocation for the file will be 50 cylinders. If the data set grows beyond that initial allocation, VSAM allocates secondary extents of 5 cylinders each. VSAM can allocate up to 122 secondary extents to the file before it must be reorganized.

For small test files, the easiest way to allocate space is to use the RECORDS parameter at the CLUSTER or DATA level. That way, you can be sure you'll allocate enough space for the records in your file. For production files, however, it's more efficient to allocate space using CYLINDERS (or BLOCKS, if you're using an FBA-type disk on a VSE system). Unfortunately, the details of calculating space requirements when you use CYLINDERS or BLOCKS are beyond the scope of this book.

Parameters that affect performance

In this section, I'll introduce you to three more DEFINE CLUSTER parameters. The IMBED parameter lets you change the way VSAM stores the index component of a key-sequenced data set. The FREESPACE parameter lets you allocate free space to the control intervals and control areas of a file. And the CONTROLINTERVALSIZE parameter lets you specify the size of the control intervals of a file.

The IMBED parameter   When you code the IMBED parameter, VSAM moves sequence set records from the space allocated to the index set and places them in the space allocated to the data component. You can code IMBED at either the CLUSTER or the INDEX level. Either way, the effect is the same. VSAM uses the first track of each control area to store the sequence set record that corresponds to that control area. As a result, VSAM can access a sequence set record and all the control intervals it indexes with a single movement, or *seek*, of the DASD's access mechanism.

In addition, coding the IMBED parameter causes VSAM to duplicate the sequence set record as many times as possible on its track. That reduces *rotational delay* when the sequence set record is read. (Rotational delay is the length of time the DASD has to wait for the desired record to pass under the read/write heads.) Even though the performance benefit of fewer seeks and less rotational delay is measured in milliseconds, it can have a significant effect on the overall performance of your application. As a result, I recommend you always code IMBED for key-sequenced data sets, even for test files.

The FREESPACE parameter   As you learned in chapter 2, you can reserve free space within the data component of a key-sequenced file. In the FREESPACE parameter, you code two values. The first value specifies the percentage of free space VSAM should reserve within each control interval. The second value specifies the percentage of control intervals within each control area VSAM should reserve as free space. I coded the FREESPACE parameter in example 1 in figure 6-5 like this:

```
FREESPACE(20 10)
```

Here, VSAM reserves 20 percent of the space in each control interval for insertions, and reserves 10 percent of the control intervals in each control area for control interval splits.

Whether or not you code this parameter, you will be able to add records to the file you're defining. But when you add a record to a file that doesn't have any free space allocated to it, VSAM must make room for the new record by performing control interval and control area splits. Since control interval and control area splits are inefficient, you should try to avoid them by coding the FREESPACE parameter for every file you define.

The CONTROLINTERVALSIZE (CISZ) parameter   One of the most important ways to insure good file performance is to select an appropriate control interval size. If you don't specify a CI size, VSAM picks one that it thinks will be optimum. Unfortunately, VSAM is almost always wrong. In fact, you're usually better off assigning a CI size of 4096 to *all* your files. For most files, 4096 is the best CI size. And even if 4096 isn't the best size, it's probably better than the CI size VSAM would have picked.

You can code the CONTROLINTERVALSIZE parameter (usually abbreviated CISZ) on the DEFINE CLUSTER command to specify the size of a file's control intervals. I coded all three examples in figure 6-5 with:

```
CISZ(4096)
```

Although you can code the CISZ parameter at the CLUSTER level, that's not a good idea. When you do, VSAM assigns the same CI size to both the data and index components. Instead, you should specify CISZ at the DATA level, and let VSAM calculate the index CI size. VSAM usually does a good job at that.

How to use the SHAREOPTIONS parameter

The SHAREOPTIONS parameter tells VSAM whether you want to let two or more jobs process a file at the same time. VSAM provides for two options in this parameter, one for cross-region sharing and one for cross-system sharing, but you should only need the cross-region option as you create and process test files.

The three values you're likely to use for the cross-region option are summarized in figure 6-4. Option 1 lets any number of jobs open a file simultaneously, as long as the file is opened for input only. Option 2 is similar, but it lets one job open the file for output and an unlimited number of jobs open the file for input at the same time. Option 3 provides no restrictions for file sharing, so any number of jobs can open the file for input or output. However, VSAM does nothing to insure the integrity of the file when you use option 3.

In a testing environment, you'll often make copies of the test files you need. If so, you won't have to use this parameter at all. Instead, you'll process your own files without sharing them.

Sometimes, though, a group of programmers will share the same test files as they develop related programs. Then, you will want to use this parameter as you define the test files. If you define a file for batch processing only, you can use option 1 or option 2. But if the file will also be processed by CICS programs, you should use option 3.

If you define a file with alternate indexes that will be processed by a COBOL program, you should code share option 3, even if the file isn't going to be shared. Because a COBOL program tries to open the base cluster more than once when alternate indexes are used, the open statement will fail unless sharing is specified. With option 3, the base cluster can be opened as many times as necessary for input or output. In figure 6-5, you can see that I specified share option 3 for the key-sequenced data set so one or more alternate indexes can be used with this file.

If you're using an MVS system, you should realize that the cross-region share options are similar to those of the DISP parameter in a DD statement. Share options 1 and 2 are similar to DISP=OLD. Share option 3 is similar to DISP=SHR. You should also realize that the share options have no meaning unless DISP=SHR is coded for a file. If DISP=OLD is coded, the file is locked out to other jobs no matter what share option is specified.

How to use the MODEL parameter or a model cluster

Many installations have standards for VSAM file parameters that you must specify for most DEFINE CLUSTER commands. To simplify this requirement, you can code the MODEL parameter to *model* your cluster after an existing cluster. To do that, just specify the name of an existing cluster in the MODEL parameter. Then, VSAM will copy any file attributes you don't specify in your DEFINE CLUSTER command from the model cluster.

On MVS systems, programmers often create special data sets to use as models. For example, you might want to define a KSDS named KSDS.MODEL to use as a model for all your key-sequenced files. Then, whenever you define a KSDS, you code this parameter at the CLUSTER level:

```
MODEL(KSDS.MODEL)
```

In this case, VSAM will take any parameters you don't code directly on your DEFINE CLUSTER command from KSDS.MODEL.

Under DOS/VSE, you can create *default models*. They are clusters with no space allocated to them that you can use as models for other clusters. Default clusters have the following reserved cluster names:

```
DEFAULT.MODEL.KSDS
DEFAULT.MODEL.ESDS
DEFAULT.MODEL.RRDS
```

If one of these default model clusters exists, you don't have to code a MODEL parameter in your DEFINE CLUSTER commands. VSAM automatically uses these entries as models.

Discussion

In this topic, I've presented a simplified version of the DEFINE CLUSTER command. So you should realize that you can code many other parameters with this command. Some of these parameters affect the efficiency with which a file can be processed; some establish password protection for a file. In general, though, you don't need any of these other parameters when you design the files that you use for program development. In fact, you'll usually define your files using a command that is similar to one of the examples in figure 6-5.

Terminology

cluster
volume serial number
vol-ser
seek
rotational delay
model
default model

Objective

Given specifications for a KSDS, ESDS, or RRDS, code an AMS job to define the cluster.

Topic 3 How to define and build alternate indexes

In this topic, you'll learn how to use AMS facilities to define and build alternate indexes. To create an alternate index for a previously defined base cluster, you issue two DEFINE commands: one to define the alternate index itself, and another to define a special catalog entry called a *path* that lets you process a base cluster via its alternate index. Then, you issue a BLDINDEX command to create the index entries that let you access base cluster records using the alternate key.

How to define an alternate index and path

To define an alternate index and its path, you code two AMS commands in an IDCAMS job: a DEFINE ALTERNATEINDEX command to define the alternate index and a DEFINE PATH command to define the path.

The DEFINE ALTERNATEINDEX command

Figure 6-8 presents the format of the DEFINE ALTERNATEINDEX command. As you can see, its format is similar to the format of the DEFINE CLUSTER command. You may remember from chapter 2 that an alternate index is actually a key-sequenced data set. As a result, you code many of the same parameters to define an alternate index that you use to define a KSDS. Since you learned how to code most of these parameters in the last topic, I'll describe just the parameters that have special meaning for alternate indexes in this topic.

Because the word ALTERNATEINDEX is long and easy to misspell, I usually code its abbreviation, AIX. In the rest of this topic, then, I'll refer to the DEFINE ALTERNATEINDEX command as the DEFINE AIX command.

The NAME parameter   You code the NAME parameter in a DEFINE AIX command to name the alternate index you're creating. To name an alternate index, I usually use a combination of the base cluster name, the alternate key field, and the abbreviation AIX. For example, if I wanted to define an alternate index for the district number field in a customer master file, I might name the alternate index as follows:

```
MMA2.CUSTMAST.DISTRICT.AIX
```

```
DEFINE {ALTERNATEINDEX} ( NAME(entry-name)
       {AIX          }   RELATE(entry-name)

                         [OWNER(owner-id)]

                         [KEYS(length offset)]

                          [{UNIQUEKEY     }]
                           {NONUNIQUEKEY  }

                          [{UPGRADE  }]
                           {NOUPGRADE }

                         VOLUMES(vol-ser...)

                          {CYLINDERS}
                          {TRACKS   }(primary [secondary])
                          {RECORDS  }
                          {BLOCKS   }

                          [{UNIQUE       }]
                           {SUBALLOCATION}

                         [FREESPACE(ci ca)]

                         [IMBED]

                         [SHAREOPTIONS(option)]

                         [MODEL(entry-name)] )

        [DATA      ( [NAME(entry-name)]

                     [VOLUMES(vol-ser...)]

                      {CYLINDERS}
                     [{TRACKS   }(primary [secondary])]
                      {RECORDS  }
                      {BLOCKS   }

                     [CONTROLINTERVALSIZE(bytes)] )

        [INDEX     ( [NAME(entry-name)]

                     [VOLUMES(vol-ser...)]

                      {CYLINDERS}
                     [{TRACKS   }(primary [secondary])] )
                      {RECORDS  }
                      {BLOCKS   }

        [CATALOG      (name)]
```

Figure 6-8   The DEFINE ALTERNATEINDEX command (part 1 of 3)

Parameter	Explanation
NAME(entry-name)	Required. Specifies the name of the alternate index or component.
RELATE(entry-name)	Required. Specifies the name of the base cluster to which this alternate index is related.
OWNER(owner-id)	Optional. Specifies the one- to eight-character owner-id for the file.
KEYS(length offset)	Optional. Specifies the length and offset of the alternate key within the base cluster.
UNIQUEKEY NONUNIQUEKEY	Optional. Specifies whether duplicate key values are allowed. NONUNIQUEKEY is the default.
UPGRADE NOUPGRADE	Optional. Specifies whether the alternate index is a part of the base cluster's upgrade set. UPGRADE is the default.
VOLUMES(vol-ser...)	Required. Specifies one or more volumes that will contain the alternate index or its components.
primary	Required. Specifies how much space to initially allocate to the alternate index or component, expressed in cylinders, tracks, records, or blocks.
secondary	Optional. Specifies the secondary space allocation amount. Ignored for unique alternate indexes under VSE.
UNIQUE SUBALLOCATION	Optional. Specifies whether the alternate index is unique or suballocated. SUBALLOCATION is the default.
FREESPACE(ci ca)	Optional. Specifies the percentage of space in each control interval and the percentage of control intervals in each control area VSAM should reserve for insertions.

Figure 6-8   The DEFINE ALTERNATEINDEX command (part 2 of 3)

Parameter	Explanation
IMBED	Optional. Moves sequence set records from the index storage area to the first track of the data storage area. Also duplicates records as many times as possible on that track.
SHAREOPTIONS(option)	Optional. The option specifies how the file (or index) may be shared. Use 1 for a file that can be processed by multiple jobs as long as no job opens the file for output. Use 2 for a file that can be processed by multiple jobs as long as only one job opens the file for output. Use 3 for a file that can be processed by multiple jobs for input or output.
MODEL(entry-name)	Optional. Specifies the name of an existing alternate index to use as a model.
CONTROLINTERVALSIZE(bytes)	Optional. Specifies size of control intervals. Abbreviated as CISZ.
CATALOG(name)	Optional. Specifies the name of the catalog that will own the alternate index. If you omit the CATALOG parameter, the stepcat, jobcat, high-level qualifier (MVS only), or master catalog identifies the catalog.

Figure 6-8   The DEFINE ALTERNATEINDEX command (part 3 of 3)

I suggest that you also code the NAME parameter at the DATA and INDEX levels of a DEFINE AIX command. That way, you can identify the data and index components of an alternate index in an output listing. For the district number alternate index, I'd name the data and index components

```
MMA2.CUSTMAST.DISTRICT.AIX.DATA
```

and

```
MMA2.CUSTMAST.DISTRICT.AIX.INDEX
```

The RELATE parameter   The RELATE parameter links an alternate index to its base cluster. In it, you code the name of the existing key-sequenced data set you're defining the alternate index for. If, for example, you're defining an alternate index for a base cluster named MMA2.CUSTMAST, you code this parameter like this:

```
RELATE(MMA2.CUSTMAST)
```

The KEYS and UNIQUEKEY/NONUNIQUEKEY parameters   To identify the alternate key and specify whether it allows duplicate keys, you code the KEYS and UNIQUEKEY/NONUNIQUEKEY parameters. The KEYS parameter specifies the length and offset of the alternate key. For example, if a five-byte alternate key is in positions 10-14 of the base cluster record, you code:

```
KEYS(5 9)
```

Remember, offset values start with zero, so the tenth byte of a record is offset 9.

UNIQUEKEY and NONUNIQUEKEY specify whether the alternate keys must be unique. The default is NONUNIQUEKEY, so if you don't want duplicate keys in your alternate index, you specify UNIQUEKEY.

The UPGRADE/NOUPGRADE parameter   In chapter 2, you learned that an alternate index may or may not be upgradable. If you want VSAM to update the alternate index whenever you make a change to the base cluster, code the UPGRADE option in the DEFINE AIX command, or allow it to default to UPGRADE. If you don't want the alternate index to be upgradable, code NOUPGRADE.

Space allocation parameters   There are three space allocation parameters. In the first parameter, VOLUMES, you specify the volume or volumes that will contain the alternate index. You can code VOLUMES at the AIX level or at the DATA and INDEX levels. You code the second parameter, the allocation parameter, the same as you code it in the DEFINE CLUSTER command. That is, you specify primary and secondary allocation in terms of RECORDS, TRACKS, CYLINDERS, or BLOCKS. In the third parameter, UNIQUE/SUBALLOCATION, you specify whether you want the alternate index to have its own space or to be suballocated out of existing VSAM space. If you're using ICF catalogs, the UNIQUE/SUBALLOCATION parameter doesn't apply.

The DEFINE PATH command

When you process the records of a base cluster via the alternate keys stored in an alternate index, you don't access the base cluster or the alternate index directly. Instead, you access them together using another catalog entry called a *path*.

To create a path, you issue the DEFINE PATH command, as shown in figure 6-9. There are just four important parameters of the DEFINE PATH command: NAME, PATHENTRY, UPDATE/NOUPDATE, and CATALOG.

```
DEFINE PATH    ( NAME(entry-name)

                 PATHENTRY(entry-name)

               [ {UPDATE  } ] )
                 {NOUPDATE}

         [CATALOG  (name)]
```

Parameter	Explanation
NAME(entry-name)	Required. Specifies the name of the path.
PATHENTRY(entry-name)	Required. Specifies the name of the alternate index to which this path is related.
UPDATE NOUPDATE	Optional. Specifies whether the upgrade set should be updated when this path is processed. UPDATE is the default.
CATALOG (name)	Optional. Specifies the name of the catalog that contains the alternate index. If you omit the CATALOG parameter, the stepcat, jobcat, high-level qualifier (MVS only), or master catalog identifies the catalog.

Figure 6-9   The DEFINE PATH command

In the PATHENTRY parameter, you specify the name you coded in the NAME parameter of the DEFINE AIX command. Then, in the NAME parameter, you supply the name of the path you're defining. To form the path name, I recommend that you use the name you coded in the PATHENTRY parameter, substituting PATH for AIX. (You'll see an example of this in a moment.) You use the CATALOG parameter to specify the catalog that will own the path.

The UPDATE/NOUPDATE parameter tells AMS whether you want VSAM to maintain the base cluster's upgrade set when you process the base cluster via the path. (An *upgrade set* consists of all of a base cluster's upgradable alternate indexes.) If you specify UPDATE, VSAM will open all the alternate indexes in the base cluster's upgrade set when you open the path. And it will maintain those upgrade set members when you process the data set. If you code NOUPDATE, VSAM does not maintain the upgrade set when you process the file via the path.

The relationship between the UPGRADE/NOUPGRADE parameter of DEFINE AIX and the UPDATE/NOUPDATE parameter of DEFINE PATH is sometimes confusing. On the DEFINE AIX command, the UPGRADE/NOUPGRADE parameter specifies whether VSAM should include the alternate index in the base cluster's upgrade set. VSAM always maintains this upgrade set when you process the base cluster via its primary key. When you use the UPDATE/NOUPDATE parameter of the DEFINE PATH command, you have additional control over whether VSAM maintains the upgrade set when you process the base cluster via an alternate key.

In most cases, I suggest you code UPDATE on your DEFINE PATH commands. Then, you can control whether alternate indexes are upgraded by coding UPGRADE or NOUPGRADE in your DEFINE AIX commands. That way, if there are any alternate indexes in the base cluster's upgrade set, they will always be maintained, whether the cluster is processed directly or via a path.

An example of the DEFINE AIX and DEFINE PATH commands

Figure 6-10 shows how you use the DEFINE AIX and DEFINE PATH commands together to define an alternate index and path. The first thing you have to do is invoke IDCAMS. I didn't code that in figure 6-10, however, because it's different for each operating system. Obviously, though, you need to invoke IDCAMS before you can process any AMS commands.

After you invoke IDCAMS, you use the DEFINE AIX command to define the alternate index. In figure 6-10, the alternate key values are employee social security numbers. The name of the alternate index is EMPMAST.FILE.SSN.AIX, and the base cluster is named EMPLOYEE.MASTER.FILE. The alternate keys are nine bytes long, starting in the thirteenth byte (offset 12) of each record. There are no duplicates (UNIQUEKEY), and this alternate index is not a part of the base cluster's upgrade set (NOUPGRADE).

Next, you use the DEFINE PATH command to define the path. In figure 6-10, the path is named EMPMAST.FILE.SSN.PATH, and it's for the alternate index named EMPMAST.FILE.SSN.AIX. Because I coded the UPDATE parameter, VSAM will maintain the base cluster's upgrade set when I process the base cluster via this path, even though this alternate index isn't part of the upgrade set.

```
DEFINE AIX    ( NAME(EMPMAST.FILE.SSN.AIX)           -
                RELATE(EMPLOYEE.MASTER.FILE)         -
                OWNER(DLOWE2)                        -
                KEYS(9 12)                           -
                UNIQUEKEY                            -
                NOUPGRADE                            -
                VOLUMES(MPS800)                      -
                UNIQUE                               -
                FREESPACE(20 10)                     -
                SHAREOPTIONS(3)                      -
                IMBED )                              -
       DATA   ( NAME(EMPMAST.FILE.SSN.AIX.DATA)      -
                CYLINDERS(1 1)                       -
                CISZ(4096) )                         -
      INDEX   ( NAME(EMPMAST.FILE.SSN.AIX.INDEX) )
DEFINE PATH   ( NAME(EMPMAST.FILE.SSN.PATH)          -
                PATHENTRY(EMPMAST.FILE.SSN.AIX)      -
                UPDATE )
```

Figure 6-10   A DEFINE ALTERNATEINDEX and DEFINE PATH command

How to build an alternate index

Once you've defined all of the alternate indexes and their paths for the
file, you need to issue a BLDINDEX command for each alternate index
to create the alternate key entries to access the base cluster. You also
need to issue the BLDINDEX command periodically to rebuild each
alternate index, even if the index is upgradable. Because VSAM makes
additions to an alternate index in the order in which they occur rather
than in primary key sequence, most alternate indexes need periodic
reorganization.

The operation of the BLDINDEX command is simple. First,
BLDINDEX reads all the records in your base cluster. From those
records, it extracts the data it needs to build your alternate index: key-
pointer pairs that consist of one alternate key value and the primary
key of the corresponding base cluster record. Then, it sorts those key-
pointer pairs into ascending alternate key sequence. Last, it writes the
pairs to your alternate index. If your alternate index allows only unique
keys, each key-pointer pair becomes one alternate index record, and
BLDINDEX flags duplicates as errors. If your alternate index allows
nonunique keys, BLDINDEX combines duplicates into a single alternate
index record.

```
BLDINDEX    {INFILE(filename)          }
            {INDATASET(entry-name)}
            {OUTFILE(ddname...)          }
            {OUTDATASET(entry-name...)}
```

Parameter	Explanation
INFILE(ddname) INDATASET(entry-name)	Required. INFILE specifies the name of a DD or DLBL statement that identifies the base cluster. INDATASET identifies the name of the base cluster itself.
OUTFILE(ddname) OUTDATASET(entry-name)	Required. OUTFILE specifies the name of a DD or DLBL statement that identifies the alternate index or path to be built. OUTDATASET identifies the name of the alternate index or path directly.

Figure 6-11   The BLDINDEX command

The BLDINDEX command

Figure 6-11 presents the format of the BLDINDEX command. Unlike the DEFINE commands, the BLDINDEX command has no parameter levels. As a result, you code all its parameters right after the word BLDINDEX.

To use the BLDINDEX command, you need to identify two VSAM files: an input file and an output file. The input file is the base cluster. The output file is always an alternate index, but you can specify either the alternate index itself or its path. Either way, VSAM processes the alternate index as the output file.

You can identify the input and output files in two ways. First, you can identify the base cluster or alternate index directly by coding its name in the INDATASET or OUTDATASET parameter. Second, you can code an INFILE or OUTFILE parameter that refers to a DD or DLBL statement that identifies the base cluster or alternate index. I prefer to use the INDATASET and OUTDATASET parameters so I don't have to code additional JCL.

For small files, such as the test files you'll use as you develop programs, VSAM uses internal memory to sort the alternate keys. For larger production files, however, there may not be enough memory available to perform an internal sort. When that happens, VSAM performs an external sort, which requires separate work files. Depending on your installation, you may or may not need to code additional parameters and JCL statements to allocate those work files. As I said, though, you

```
BLDINDEX INDATASET(MMA2.EMPLOYEE.MASTER)      -
         OUTDATASET(MMA2.EMPMAST.SSN.AIX)
```

Figure 6-12   A BLDINDEX command

don't need to worry about it for small files. Since VSAM can perform the sort internally, no work files are required

Examples of the BLDINDEX command

Figure 6-12 shows a sample BLDINDEX command. Here, I assume that the file is small enough that the sort can be performed internally. For larger files, you would have to code additional parameters and JCL statements to allow an external sort.

Discussion

As I explained in chapter 2, you usually don't use COBOL programs to process files with alternate indexes. However, you also use the AMS commands I presented in this topic when you use alternate indexes with files that are going to be processed by CICS or assembler language programs. So one way or another, the commands in this topic will probably come in handy.

Terminology

path
upgrade set

Objective

Given specifications for a key-sequenced data set and its alternate index, code the required AMS commands to define the alternate index, to define the path, and to build the alternate index.

Topic 4   Catalog maintenance functions

In this topic, you'll learn how to use three AMS commands for maintaining catalogs: LISTCAT, ALTER, and DELETE. The LISTCAT command lets you list the contents of a catalog. The ALTER command lets you change the characteristics of an existing VSAM file. And the DELETE command lets you delete a VSAM file by removing its catalog entry.

The LISTCAT command

Often, you need to know what VSAM files are defined in a particular user catalog or what the characteristics of a particular file are. To get that information, you use the LISTCAT command, presented in figure 6-13. The parameters you code in the LISTCAT command identify the catalog, the names of the entries to list, the types of objects to list, and the amount of information to list about each object.

Identifying the catalog   The first LISTCAT parameter, CATALOG, names the catalog whose contents you want to list. If you omit the CATALOG parameter, VSAM uses its standard search order to determine which catalog to use. Under VSE, I recommend you always code the CATALOG parameter in your LISTCAT commands. That way, you'll know for sure what catalog you're listing. Under MVS, however, you'll normally omit the CATALOG parameter since the high-level qualifier of each file name determines the correct user catalog.

Identifying the entries to be listed   The next two parameters, ENTRIES and LEVEL, identify the catalog entries you want to list. Under MVS, you can code ENTRIES or LEVEL to identify the catalog entries, and you can code *generic entry names* to cause VSAM to list more than one entry. (I'll explain what generic entry names are in a moment.) Under VSE, however, you can't code the LEVEL parameter or generic names; VSE allows only the ENTRIES parameter.

The ENTRIES parameter lets you specify one or more names for the catalog entries you want listed. For example, if you want to list the catalog entry for a VSAM file named CUSTOMER.MASTER.FILE, you code

```
ENTRIES(CUSTOMER.MASTER.FILE)
```

```
LISTCAT   [CATALOG(name)]

          [ {ENTRIES(entry-name...)}  ]
            {LEVEL(level)          }

          [entry-type]

            /NAME      \
            |HISTORY   |
          [ {VOLUME    } ]
            |ALLOCATION|
            \ALL       /
```

Figure 6-13   The LISTCAT command (part 1 of 2)

To list information for more than one file, just code several file names in
a single ENTRIES parameter, like this:

```
ENTRIES ( CUSTOMER.MASTER.FILE      -
          EMPLOYEE.MASTER.FILE      -
          DAILY.TRANS.FILE )
```

Here, VSAM will list three catalog entries.

On MVS systems, you can specify a generic entry name by replacing
one or more levels of the file name with an asterisk. For example, if you
code

```
ENTRIES(MMA2.*.MASTER)
```

VSAM will list all files whose names consist of three levels with MMA2
as the first level and MASTER as the third level. The files named
MMA2.CUSTOMER.MASTER and MMA2.EMPLOYEE.MASTER meet
these criteria. The level represented by the asterisk in a generic name
must be present for an entry to be listed, however. So, in this example,
VSAM would not list MMA2.MASTER because the second level of the
entry name is missing.

The LEVEL parameter is similar to generic entry names in an
ENTRIES parameter. In the LEVEL parameter, you code a partial
name consisting of one or more levels. VSAM then lists all the catalog
entries whose names begin with the partial name. For example, if you
code

```
LEVEL(MMA2)
```

Parameter	Explanation
CATALOG(name)	Optional. Specifies the name of the catalog whose entries you want to list.
ENTRIES(entry-name...)	Optional. Specifies the names of the entries you want to list. Under MVS, entry names may be generic (see text). If you omit the ENTRIES parameter, VSAM lists all the entries in the specified catalog.
LEVEL(level)	Optional. Specifies one or more levels of qualification. VSAM lists any data sets whose names match those levels. (MVS only)
entry-type	Optional. Specifies the type of entries you want listed. If you omit both ENTRIES/LEVEL and entry-type, VSAM lists all entries of all types in the specified catalog. Valid entry types include: ALTERNATEINDEX, CLUSTER, DATA, INDEX, NONVSAM, PATH, and USERCATALOG.
NAME	Optional. Specifies that VSAM should list only the names and types of the specified entries. NAME is the default.
HISTORY	Optional. Specifies that VSAM should list the information listed by NAME, plus the history information (such as creation and expiration dates). (MVS only)
VOLUME	Optional. Specifies that VSAM should list the information listed by HISTORY, plus the volume locations of the specified entries.
ALLOCATION	Optional. Specifies that VSAM should list the information listed by VOLUME, plus detailed extent information.
ALL	Optional. Specifies that VSAM should list all available catalog information for the specified entries.

Figure 6-13   The LISTCAT command (part 2 of 2)

VSAM will list all catalog entries whose first level is MMA2. In this example, it doesn't matter how many levels are actually present in the entry name, as long as the first level is MMA2.

Similarly, if you code

```
LEVEL(MMA2.EMPLOYEE)
```

Component name	Example				
	1	2	3	4	5
MMA2.CUSTOMER	X				X
MMA2.CUSTOMER.MASTER			X		X
MMA2.EMPLOYEE				X	X
MMA2.EMPLOYEE.MASTER		X	X	X	X
MMA2.EMPLOYEE.FILE		X		X	X

Example 1

```
LISTCAT ENTRIES(MMA2.CUSTOMER)
```

Example 2

```
LISTCAT ENTRIES(MMA2.EMPLOYEE.*)
```

Example 3

```
LISTCAT ENTRIES(MMA2.*.MASTER)
```

Example 4

```
LISTCAT LEVEL(MMA2.EMPLOYEE)
```

Example 5

```
LISTCAT LEVEL(MMA2)
```

Figure 6-14   Examples of the ENTRIES and LEVEL parameters of the LISTCAT command

VSAM will list any entry whose name begins with MMA2.EMPLOYEE no matter how many additional levels are in its name.

To understand how the ENTRIES and LEVEL parameters work, look at figure 6-14. Here, I've coded five LISTCAT commands that use the ENTRIES or LEVEL parameter. Then, I've shown which of the file names each of the five commands would select. If you study this figure for a moment, you'll understand the difference between the ENTRIES and LEVEL parameters.

If you omit the ENTRIES or LEVEL parameters, VSAM lists all the objects in the catalog. You'll rarely want to do that, however, since user catalogs can contain hundreds of entries.

Identifying the entry types to be listed   The third LISTCAT parameter, entry-type, lets you specify which types of catalog entries you want VSAM to list: clusters, alternate indexes, and so on. If you omit the entry-type parameter, VSAM will list all the entries that match the ENTRIES or LEVEL parameter.

You can code more than one type in a LISTCAT command. For example, if you want to list clusters and alternate indexes, you code both CLUSTER and ALTERNATEINDEX on the LISTCAT command.

Limiting the amount of catalog information to be listed   The next LISTCAT parameter lets you limit the amount of catalog information VSAM lists for each entry. If you specify NAME, or let it default, VSAM lists just the entry's name, type, and owning catalog. To illustrate, figure 6-15 shows the VSE output from this command:

```
LISTCAT CATALOG(TIM.USER.CATALOG) -
        NAME
```

As you can see, VSAM lists the names of all the files in the specified catalog as a result of this command. Under MVS, this output looks slightly different, but contains the same information.

If you specify a particular file and code VOLUMES instead of NAME, VSAM will list the same information as when you code NAME, plus the history and volume information for the data and index components. If you're using an MVS system, VSAM will also give the device type in a coded format. To determine what type of device the file resides on, look up the device code in figure 6-16. If you specify ALLOCATION instead of VOLUMES, VSAM will give you more detailed volume, allocation, and extent information for the file.

If you want to know all the characteristics of a VSAM file, specify the ALL parameter. Then, the output looks like figure 6-17. As you can see, this output can be lengthy. If you run a job to print all the entries in a typical user catalog and you specify ALL, the output can easily be hundreds of pages long. So be as specific as you can about the information you need when you run an AMS LISTCAT job. The less output you request, the simpler it will be for you to read and the less system time it will take to create and print.

```
IDCAMS   SYSTEM SERVICES
            LISTCAT CATALOG(TIM.USER.CATALOG) -
            NAME

                                    LISTING FROM CATALOG -- TIM.USER.CATALOG
VOLUME -------- DOSEXT
CLUSTER ------- EMP.MASTER.FILE
    DATA ------- EMP.MASTER.FILE.DATA
    INDEX ------ EMP.MASTER.FILE.INDEX
CLUSTER ------- EMP.TRANS.FILE
    DATA ------- EMP.TRANS.FILE.DATA
CLUSTER ------- EMPLOYEE.TRANS.FILE
    DATA ------- EMPLOYEE.TRANS.FILE.DATA
CLUSTER ------- ERROR.TRANS.FILE
    DATA ------- ERROR.TRANS.FILE.DATA
CLUSTER ------- INV.LOCATION.FILE
    DATA ------- INV.LOCATION.FILE.DATA
    INDEX ------ INV.LOCATION.FILE.INDEX
CLUSTER ------- INV.MASTER.FILE
    DATA ------- INV.MASTER.FILE.DATA
CLUSTER ------- INV.MASTERI.FILE
    DATA ------- INV.MASTERI.FILE.DATA
    INDEX ------ INV.MASTERI.FILE.INDEX
CLUSTER ------- INV.MASTR.FILE
    DATA ------- INV.MASTR.FILE.DATA
CLUSTER ------- INV.TRAN.FILE
    DATA ------- INV.TRAN.FILE.DATA
CLUSTER ------- NEW.MASTER.FILE
    DATA ------- NEW.MASTER.FILE.DATA
CLUSTER ------- OPEN.ITEM.FILE
    DATA ------- OPEN.ITEM.FILE.DATA
    INDEX ------ OPEN.ITEM.FILE.INDEX
AIX ----------- OPEN.ITEM.FILE.CNUM.AIX
    DATA ------- OPEN.ITEM.FILE.CNUM.AIX.DATA
    INDEX ------ OPEN.ITEM.FILE.CNUM.AIX.INDEX
    PATH ------- OPEN.ITEM.FILE.CNUM.PATH
CLUSTER ------- TIM.USER.CATALOG
    DATA ------- VSAM.CATALOG.BASE.DATA.RECORD
    INDEX ------ VSAM.CATALOG.BASE.INDEX.RECORD
CLUSTER ------- VAL.TRAN.FILE
    DATA ------- VAL.TRAN.FILE.DATA
CLUSTER ------- VAL.TRANS.FILE
    DATA ------- VAL.TRANS.FILE.DATA
CLUSTER ------- VALID.TRANS.FILE
    DATA ------- VALID.TRANS.FILE.DATA
```

Figure 6-15   Output from a LISTCAT command with the NAME parameter

Device code in LISTCAT output	Device type
30008001	9 track tape
3040200A	3340 (35 or 70 MB)
30502006	2305-1
30502007	2305-2
30502009	3330
3050200B	3350
3050200D	3330-1
30582009	3330 MSS virtual volume
30808001	7 track tape
30C02008	2314 or 2319
3010200C	3375
3010200E	3380
32008003	9 track, 6250 bpi tape
34008003	9 track, 1600 bpi tape

Figure 6-16   Device codes that appear in LISTCAT output

The ALTER command

Figure 6-18 presents the format of the ALTER command. With this command, you can change a VSAM file's name and other characteristics that you assigned to the file when you defined it.

Besides the parameters shown in figure 6-18, you can also code many DEFINE parameters in the ALTER command. For example, you can use an ALTER command to change the FREESPACE specification for a key-sequenced data set. Unfortunately, there are many restrictions on how you can code those parameters. As a result, I won't describe them in detail here. If you ever need them, I suggest you consult the appropriate AMS reference manual to see how to use those parameters on your system.

How to change an object's name   Example 1 in figure 6-19 shows how to change a *VSAM object's* name. (A VSAM object can be a cluster, an index or data component, an alternate index, a path, or a catalog.) To change a VSAM object's name, you code two parameters in the ALTER command: the name of the existing VSAM object and, in the NEWNAME parameter, the new name for the object.

```
IDCAMS  SYSTEM SERVICES

        LISTCAT CATALOG(TIM.USER.CATALOG)     -
                ENTRIES(EMP.MASTER.FILE)      -
                ALL
                      LISTING FROM CATALOG -- TIM.USER.CATALOG

CLUSTER ------ EMP.MASTER.FILE
     HISTORY
          OWNER-IDENT-----(NULL)          CREATION--------89.097
          RELEASE---------2               EXPIRATION------00.000
          PROTECTION------(NULL)
     ASSOCIATIONS
          DATA-----EMP.MASTER.FILE.DATA
          INDEX----EMP.MASTER.FILE.INDEX
DATA ------ EMP.MASTER.FILE.DATA
     HISTORY
          OWNER-IDENT-----(NULL)          CREATION--------89.097
          RELEASE---------2               EXPIRATION------00.000
          PROTECTION------(NULL)
     ASSOCIATIONS
          CLUSTER--EMP.MASTER.FILE
     ATTRIBUTES
          KEYLEN----------5   AVGLRECL--------103   BUFSPACE--------4608    CISIZE----------2048
          RKP-------------0   MAXLRECL--------103   EXCPEXIT--------(NULL)  CI/CA-----------8
          SHROPTNS(3,3)  RECOVERY   SUBALLOC  NOERASE   INDEXED  NOWRITECHK   NOIMBED  NOREPLICAT
          UNORDERED  NONSPANNED
     STATISTICS
          REC-TOTAL-------6   SPLITS-CI-------0    EXCPS-----------10
          REC-DELETED-----0   SPLITS-CA-------0    EXTENTS---------1
          REC-INSERTED----0   FREESPACE-%CI---0    SYSTEM-TIMESTAMP:
          REC-UPDATED-----0   FREESPACE-%CA---0        X'A020774DAD8C0000'
          REC-RETRIEVED---32  FREESPC-BYTES---0
     ALLOCATION
          SPACE-TYPE------BLOCK    USECLASS-PRI----0    HI-ALLOC-RBA----16384
          SPACE-PRI-------32      USECLASS-SEC----0    HI-USED-RBA-----16384
          SPACE-SEC-------32
     VOLUME
          VOLSER----------DOSEXT   BLKS/MIN-CA-----32    HI-ALLOC-RBA----16384   EXTENT-NUMBER---1
          DEVTYPE---------FBA      BLOCKS/CA-------32    HI-USED-RBA-----16384   EXTENT-TYPE-----X'00'
          VOLFLAG---------PRIME
          EXTENTS:
          LOW-BLOCK-------41888    LOW-RBA---------0     BLOCKS----------32
          HIGH-BLOCK------41919    HIGH-RBA--------16383
INDEX ------ EMP.MASTER.FILE.INDEX
     HISTORY
          OWNER-IDENT-----(NULL)          CREATION--------89.097
          RELEASE---------2               EXPIRATION------00.000
          PROTECTION------(NULL)
     ASSOCIATIONS
          CLUSTER--EMP.MASTER.FILE
     ATTRIBUTES
          KEYLEN----------5   AVGLRECL--------0     BUFSPACE--------0       CISIZE----------512
          RKP-------------0   MAXLRECL--------505   EXCPEXIT--------(NULL)  CI/CA-----------32
          SHROPTNS(3,3)  RECOVERY   SUBALLOC  NOERASE   NOWRITECHK   NOIMBED   NOREPLICAT  UNORDERED
          NOREUSE
     STATISTICS
          REC-TOTAL-------1   SPLITS-CI-------0    EXCPS-----------10    INDEX:
```

Figure 6-17   Output from a LISTCAT command with the ALL parameter (part 1 of 2)

```
REC-DELETED----------0   SPLITS-CA-----------0   EXTENTS-------------1   LEVELS-------------1
REC-INSERTED---------0   FREESPACE-%CI-------0   SYSTEM-TIMESTAMP:       ENTRIES/SECT-------2
REC-UPDATED----------0   FREESPACE-%CA-------0     X'A020774E287B0000'   SEQ-SET-RBA--------0
REC-RETRIEVED--------0   FREESPC-BYTES---15872                           HI-LEVEL-RBA-------0
ALLOCATION
  SPACE-TYPE------BLOCK
  SPACE-PRI----------32  USECLASS-PRI--------0   HI-ALLOC-RBA----16384
  SPACE-SEC----------32  USECLASS-SEC--------0   HI-USED-RBA-------512
VOLUME
  VOLSER--------DOSEXT
  DEVTYPE---------FBA    BLKS/MIN-CA--------32   HI-ALLOC-RBA----16384   EXTENT-NUMBER------1
  VOLFLAG-------PRIME    BLOCKS/CA----------32   HI-USED-RBA-------512   EXTENT-TYPE----X'00'
  EXTENTS:
  LOW-BLOCK------42976   LOW-RBA-------------0
  HIGH-BLOCK-----43007   HIGH-RBA-------16383   BLOCKS------------32
```

Figure 6-17   Output from a LISTCAT command with the ALL parameter (part 2 of 2)

```
ALTER   entry-name
        [CATALOG(name)]
        [NEWNAME(entry-name)]
        [ADDVOLUMES(vol-ser...)]
        [REMOVEVOLUMES(vol-ser...)]
```

Parameter	Explanation
entry-name	Required. Specifies the name of the object whose catalog entry you want to alter.
CATALOG(name)	Optional. Identifies the catalog that contains the object you want to alter. Required only if VSAM can't locate the catalog by the standard search sequence.
NEWNAME(entry-name)	Optional. Specifies a new entry name for the entry.

Figure 6-18   The ALTER command

Example 1

```
ALTER   CUSTOMER.MASTER.FILE          -
        NEWNAME(CUSTMAST.FILE)
```

Example 2

```
ALTER   CUSTOMER.MASTER.FILE.DATA     -
        ADDVOLUMES(VOL291 VOL292)     -
        REMOVEVOLUMES(VOL281 VOL282)
```

Figure 6-19   Examples of the ALTER command

The DELETE command

You use the DELETE command to remove entries from a VSAM catalog. Its format, shown in figure 6-20, is simple. To delete a VSAM file, all you normally need to include in the DELETE command is the name of the file. To delete more than one file, you list the names in parentheses. And if you want to delete the file whether or not its retention period has

```
DELETE     entry-name...
           [CATALOG(name)]
           [entry-type]
         [ {PURGE  } ]
         [ {NOPURGE } ]
```

Parameter	Explanation
entry-name...	Required. Specifies the name of the entry or entries you want to delete. If you specify more than one entry name, you must enclose the list in parentheses.
CATALOG(name)	Optional. Specifies the name of the catalog that owns the entries you want to delete. Required only if the correct catalog can't be found using the standard search sequence.
entry-type	Optional. Specifies that VSAM should only delete entries of the listed types. The valid entry types are the same as for the LISTCAT command.
PURGE NOPURGE	Optional. PURGE means VSAM should delete the object even if its retention period has not expired. NOPURGE means VSAM should delete entries only if their retention periods have expired. NOPURGE is the default.

Figure 6-20   The DELETE command

expired, code PURGE as well. The CATALOG parameter lets you specify the catalog that owns the file you want to delete. If you omit it, VSAM uses its normal search sequence.

On an MVS system, you can use a generic name in a DELETE command by replacing one level of the entry name with an asterisk, like this:

```
DELETE MMA2.CUSTOMER.*
```

Here, VSAM will delete all entries whose names consist of three levels, with the first two levels being MMA2.CUSTOMER. That includes MMA2.CUSTOMER.MASTER, MMA2.CUSTOMER.HISTORY, and so on.

The entry-type parameter lets you limit the delete operation to certain types of VSAM objects. The values you can code here are the same as the entry-types you can code in a LISTCAT command. Normally, you don't need to specify an entry-type since the names you

Example 1

```
DELETE  MMA2.CUSTOMER.MASTER                    -
        PURGE
```

Example 2

```
DELETE  (INV.TRANS.FILE                         -
         OPEN.ITEM.FILE                         -
         NEW.MASTER.FILE)
```

Example 3

```
DELETE  MMA2.CUSTMAST.*.AIX                      -
        ALTERNATEINDEX
```

Figure 6-21   Examples of the DELETE command

specify indicate which objects you want deleted. But if you use a generic name, you might want to specify that you want VSAM to delete only objects of certain types.

Figure 6-21 shows three examples of the DELETE command. In example 1, I deleted a single file named MMA2.CUSTOMER.MASTER. Because I specified the PURGE parameter, VSAM will delete this file whether or not its expiration date has arrived.

Examples 2 and 3 show how to delete several files with a single DELETE command. In example 2, I listed three names in the command. In example 3, I used a generic file name to delete all alternate indexes whose names follow the form MMA2.CUSTMAST.*.AIX.

Discussion

The LISTCAT command will help you keep track of your test files, and the DELETE command will help you maintain them. Although you should only need the ALTER command occasionally as you develop programs, it too can come in handy as you test programs.

Terminology

generic entry name
VSAM object
candidate volume

Objective

Given specifications for an AMS job requiring the LISTCAT, ALTER, or
DELETE commands, code a job stream using the options presented in
this topic.

Topic 5   How to print and copy data sets

As you test programs that process VSAM files, you'll often want to print and copy data sets. To do that, you use the AMS commands PRINT and REPRO. The formats of the two commands are similar. I'll cover PRINT first because it's a bit simpler; then I'll discuss REPRO.

The PRINT command

Figure 6-22 presents the format of the PRINT command. To identify the file you want to print, you must always code at least one parameter, INFILE or INDATASET. If you code INFILE, you specify the name of a file identified in the JCL with a DD or DLBL statement. If you code INDATASET, you supply the VSAM file name. Please note that if you are using a VSE system, you must code the INFILE parameter. The INDATASET parameter is invalid on VSE systems.

The CHARACTER, HEX, and DUMP parameters let you determine the format of the printed output. If you specify CHARACTER, AMS prints the actual characters contained in each file record. Many files contain unprintable characters like packed-decimal fields, however. You should specify HEX or DUMP for those files. HEX prints the hexadecimal value of each byte in the file's records, and DUMP prints both the character and the hex values. If you omit the parameter, the default format is DUMP.

The next two sets of parameters let you select which records you want to print. AMS starts printing at the beginning of the data set unless you specify where printing should start by coding SKIP, FROMKEY, FROMNUMBER, or FROMADDRESS. For any type of file, you can use SKIP to bypass a specified number of records. To begin printing with the 50th record, for example, code SKIP(49). For a KSDS, you can code FROMKEY with the key value of the first record you want to print. For an RRDS, you can code FROMNUMBER with the relative record number of the first record you want to print. And, for an ESDS or a KSDS, you can specify a relative byte address in the FROMADDRESS parameter.

AMS continues printing until it reaches the end of the data set unless you code COUNT, TOKEY, TONUMBER, or TOADDRESS to specify where printing should end. COUNT indicates how many records you want to print; it's valid for any type of file. For a KSDS, you use TOKEY to indicate where to stop printing. For an RRDS, you use

```
PRINT      {INFILE(input-file-name)}
           {INDATASET(entry-name) }

              {CHARACTER}
           [  {HEX      }  ]
              {DUMP     }

              {SKIP(count)          }
              {FROMKEY(key)         }
           [  {FROMNUMBER(number)   }  ]
              {FROMADDRESS(address) }

              {COUNT(count)      }
              {TOKEY(key)        }
           [  {TONUMBER(number)  }  ]
              {TOADDRESS(address)}
```

Parameter	Explanation
INFILE(input-file-name) INDATASET(entry-name)	Required. INFILE specifies the name of a DD or DLBL statement that identifies the file you want to print. INDATASET specifies the file name of the VSAM file you want to print. INDATASET is invalid on VSE systems.
CHARACTER HEX DUMP	Optional. Specifies the format of the output. CHARACTER and HEX print the data in character or hex format. DUMP prints data in both character and hex format. DUMP is the default.
SKIP(count) FROMKEY(key) FROMNUMBER(number) FROMADDRESS(address)	Optional. Specifies the first record of the file you want to print. For count, specify a numeric value to indicate the number of records to skip before printing begins. Valid for all file types. For key, specify the value of the key where printing should begin. Valid only for a KSDS. For number, specify the relative record number where printing should begin. Valid only for an RRDS. For address, specify the RBA of the first record you want to print. Valid only for a KSDS or ESDS.
COUNT(count) TOKEY(key) TONUMBER(number) TOADDRESS(address)	Optional. Specifies the last record of the file you want to print. Count specifies the number of records to be printed, and it is valid for all files. See explanation above for explanations of the key, number, and address parameters.

Figure 6-22   The PRINT command

TONUMBER to do the same thing. And for an ESDS or KSDS, you can specify a relative byte address in the TOADDRESS parameter.

Figure 6-23 presents the AMS output from the following PRINT command:

```
PRINT   INDATASET (EMP.MASTER.FILE) -
        CHARACTER                    -
        SKIP(28)                     -
        COUNT(3)
```

Notice here that I coded SKIP(28) to bypass the first 28 records and COUNT(3) to print only three records. As a result, this job prints the 29th, 30th, and 31st records in the file. Notice also that I specified the CHARACTER print format.

Figures 6-24 and 6-25 show the AMS output from the same data set and same PRINT command, but with the HEX and DUMP print formats.

The REPRO command

You use the REPRO command to copy the contents of one data set into another. Figure 6-26 presents the format of the REPRO command. As you can see, you must specify an output file on the REPRO command as well as an input file. You can do that by coding the OUTFILE or OUTDATASET parameter. If you code OUTFILE, you must specify the name of a DD or DLBL statement in the JCL that identifies the file. If you code OUTDATASET, you provide the VSAM file name. Please note that if you are using a VSE system, you must use the OUTFILE parameter. The OUTDATASET parameter is invalid on VSE systems.

If the output file doesn't exist, you must define it using the DEFINE CLUSTER command before VSAM can perform the REPRO command. When the output file is empty, VSAM processes the file in load mode and copies the records one by one from the input file to the output file. But when the output file is not empty, VSAM merges records from the input file with the records in the output file. For an ESDS, VSAM adds records at the end of the output file. For a KSDS or RRDS, VSAM adds records at the correct position based on key values or relative record numbers.

VSAM handles duplicates according to how you code the REPLACE option. If you specify REPLACE, duplicates in the input file replace existing records in the output file. If you specify NOREPLACE, they do not.

You can use the SKIP, FROMKEY, FROMNUMBER, and FROMADDRESS parameters along with the COUNT, TOKEY, TONUMBER, and TOADDRESS parameters to limit the number of

```
IDCAMS  SYSTEM  SERVICES

LISTING OF DATA SET -EMP.MASTER.FILE

KEY OF RECORD - 00404
00404MAXINE      EHOUVARDAS        98454586730 N. ROOSEVELT AVE.    FRESNO      CA93725

KEY OF RECORD - 00407
00407JIM         CDENNING          84559674457135 N. FRUIT          FRESNO      CA93711

KEY OF RECORD - 00695
00695VINCENTE  ACRUZ               48967645432S5 W. CHURCH ST.      CLOVIS      CA93612
```

Figure 6-23   Output from a PRINT command with the CHARACTER parameter

```
IDCAMS  SYSTEM  SERVICES

LISTING OF DATA SET -EMP.MASTER.FILE

KEY OF RECORD - F0F0F4F0F4
F0F0F4F0F4D4C1E7C9D5C540404040C5C8D6E4E5C1D9C4C1E24040404040404040404040404040F9F8F4F5F3F4F5F8F6F7F3F04OD54B4OD9D6D6E2C5E5C5D3
E340C1E5C54B4040404040404040C6D9C5E2D5D640404040404040404040404040404040404040C3C1F9F3F7F2F5

KEY OF RECORD - F0F0F4F0F7
F0F0F4F0F7D1C9D4404040404040C3C4C5D5D5C9D5C740404040404040404040F8F4F5F5F9F6F7F4F5F7F1F3F540D54B40C6D9E4C9E34040
40404040404040404040404040404040404040404040404040C6D9C5E2D5D640404040404040404040404040404040404040C3C1F9F3F7F1F1

KEY OF RECORD - F0F0F6F9F5
F0F0F6F9F5E5C9D5C3C5D5E3C540404040C1C3D9E4E940404040404040404040F4F8F9F6F7F6F4F5F4F3F2F540E64B40C3C8E4D9C3C840
E2E34B404040404040404040C3D3D6E5C9E240404040404040404040404040404040404040404040C3C1F9F3F6F1F2
```

Figure 6-24   Output from a PRINT command with the HEX parameter

```
IDCAMS  SYSTEM  SERVICES

LISTING OF DATA SET -EMP.MASTER.FILE

KEY OF RECORD - F0F0F4F0F4
0000  F0F0F4F0 F4D4C1E7 C9D5C540 404040C5   C8D6E4E5 C1D9C4C1 E2404040 40404040   *00404MAXINE    EHOUVARDAS    *
0020  40404040 F9F8F4F5 F3F4F5F8 F6F7F3F0   40D54B40 D9D6D6E2 C5E34040 E340C1E5   *    984534586730 N. ROOSEVELT AV*
0040  C54B4040 40404040 40404OC6 D9C5E2D5   D6404040 40404040 40404040 40404040   *E.      FRESNO              *
0060  C3C1F9F3 F7F2F5                                                             *CA93725                      *

KEY OF RECORD - F0F0F4F0F7
0000  F0F0F4F0 F7D1C9D4 40404040 404040C3   C4C5D5D5 C9D5C740 40404040 40404040   *00407JIM    CDENNING        *
0020  40404040 F8F4F5F5 F9F6F7F4 F5F7F1F3   F540D54B 40C6D9E4 C9E34040 40404040   *    845967457135 N. FRUIT   *
0040  40404040 40404040 40404OC6 D9C5E2D5   D6404040 40404040 40404040 40404040   *          FRESNO            *
0060  C3C1F9F3 F7F1F1                                                             *CA93711                      *

KEY OF RECORD - F0F0F6F9F5
0000  F0F0F6F9 F5E5C9D5 C3C5D5E3 C54040C1   C3D9E4E9 40404040 40404040 40404040   *00695VINCENTE ACRUZ        *
0020  40404040 F4F8F9F6 F7F6F4F5 F4F3F2F5   F540E64B 40C3C8E4 D9C3C840 E2E34B40   *    489676454325 W. CHURCH ST. *
0040  40404040 40404040 40404OC3 D3D6E5C9   E2404040 40404040 40404040 40404040   *          CLOVIS           *
0060  C3C1F9F3 F6F1F2                                                             *CA93612                      *
```

Figure 6-25   Output from a PRINT command with the DUMP parameter

```
REPRO     (INFILE(input-file-name)|
          |INDATASET(entry-name)  )

          (OUTFILE(output-file-name)|
          |OUTDATASET(entry-name)   )

            (SKIP(count)            )
          [ |FROMKEY(key)           | ]
            |FROMNUMBER(number)     |
            (FROMADDRESS(address)   )

            (COUNT(count)           )
          [ |TOKEY(key)             | ]
            |TONUMBER(number)       |
            (TOADDRESS(address)     )

            (REPLACE  )
          [ |NOREPLACE| ]
```

Figure 6-26   The REPRO command (part 1 of 2)

---

records copied. You code these parameters just like you do for a PRINT command.

If you wish, the input and output files can be of different types. In other words, you can copy an ESDS input file to a RRDS output file. Or, you can copy an ISAM file to a KSDS. There's no restriction on the combination of input and output file types, except that you can't specify an ISAM file as the output file.

Figure 6-27 shows three examples of the REPRO command. In example 1, I used the INFILE and OUTFILE parameters to identify the input and output files. In example 2, I used the INDATASET and OUTDATASET parameters. In example 3, I used the COUNT parameter to limit the copy operation to 10 records.

One of the most common uses of the REPRO command is for reorganizing key-sequenced data sets. When REPRO opens a KSDS for output and loads it, VSAM restores the free space you originally allocated and consolidates the file into a single extent, if possible.

Figure 6-28 shows the typical AMS commands you'll use to reorganize a KSDS. First, you code a DEFINE CLUSTER command to define the new file, using the existing file as a model. Next, you code a REPRO command to copy data from the old KSDS to the new one. Then, you code a DELETE command to delete the old KSDS. Finally, you code ALTER commands to change the names of the new KSDS and its data and index components back to their original names.

Parameter	Explanation
INFILE(input-file-name) INDATASET(entry-name)	Required. INFILE specifies the name of a DD or DLBL statement that identifies the file you want to copy. INDATASET specifies the name of the data set you want to copy. INDATASET is an invalid parameter for VSE systems.
OUTFILE(output-file-name) OUTDATASET(entry-name)	Required. OUTFILE specifies the name of a DD or DLBL statement that identifies the file you want to copy the input file to. OUTDATASET specifies the name of the data set you want to copy the input file to. OUTDATASET is an invalid parameter for VSE systems.
SKIP(count) FROMKEY(key) FROMNUMBER(number) FROMADDRESS(address)	Optional. Specifies the first record of the file you want to copy. For count, specify a numeric value to indicate the number of records to skip before copying begins. Valid for all file types. For key, specify the value of the key where copying should begin. Valid only for a KSDS. For number, specify the relative record number where copying should begin. Valid only for an RRDS. For address, specify the RBA of the first record you want to copy. Valid only for a KSDS or ESDS.
COUNT(count) TOKEY(key) TONUMBER(number) TOADDRESS(address)	Optional. Specifies the last record of the file you want to copy. See explanation above for the count, key, number, and address parameters.
REPLACE NOREPLACE	Optional. Specifies how VSAM should handle duplicate records. If you specify REPLACE, VSAM replaces duplicate records; if you specify NOREPLACE, VSAM treats duplicates as errors. NOREPLACE is the default.

Figure 6-26   The REPRO command (part 2 of 2)

Discussion

You should find many uses for the PRINT and REPRO commands as you create and use test files. As I've explained, you can use these commands for both VSAM and non-VSAM files. The primary limitation is that you can't use REPRO to create an ISAM file.

Example 1:   Copying the data set identified by the CUSTMST DD or DLBL statement to the data set identified by the CUSTCPY DD or DLBL statement.

```
REPRO  INFILE(CUSTMST) -
       OUTFILE(CUSTCPY)
```

Example 2:   Copying MMA2.CUSTOMER.MASTER to MMA2.CUSTOMER.MASTER.COPY. (Not valid on VSE systems.)

```
REPRO  INDATASET(MMA2.CUSTOMER.MASTER) -
       OUTDATASET(MMA2.CUSTOMER.MASTER.COPY)
```

Example 3:   Copying the first 10 records of the data set identified by the CUSTMST DD or DLBL statement to the data set identified by the CUSTCPY DD or DLBL statement

```
REPRO  INFILE(CUSTMST)    -
       OUTFILE(CUSTCPY)   -
       COUNT(10)
```

Figure 6-27   Three examples of the REPRO command

Objective

Given specifications for a printing or copying job, code the required PRINT or REPRO command using the options presented in this topic.

```
DEFINE  CLUSTER ( NAME(MMA2.EMPMAST.REPRO)            -
                  MODEL(MMA2.EMPLOYEE.MASTER)         -
                  VOLUMES(MPS8BV) )                   -
        DATA    ( NAME(MMA2.EMPMAST.REPRO.DATA)       -
                  CYLINDERS(5 1) )                    -
        INDEX   ( NAME(MMA2.EMPMAST.REPRO.INDEX) )
REPRO   INDATASET(MMA2.EMPLOYEE.MASTER)               -
        OUTDATASET(MMA2.EMPMAST.REPRO)
DELETE  MMA2.EMPLOYEE.MASTER
ALTER   MMA2.EMPMAST.REPRO                            -
        NEWNAME(MMA2.EMPLOYEE.MASTER)
ALTER   MMA2.EMPMAST.REPRO.DATA                       -
        NEWNAME(MMA2.EMPLOYEE.MASTER.DATA)
ALTER   MMA2.EMPMAST.REPRO.INDEX                      -
        NEWNAME(MMA2.EMPLOYEE.MASTER.INDEX)
```

Figure 6-28   AMS commands to reorganize a VSAM key-sequenced data set

Index

An expanded VSAM book from Mike Murach & Associates

VSAM

Access Method Services and Application Programming   **Doug Lowe**

As its title suggests, *VSAM: Access Method Services and Application Programming* has two main purposes: (1) to teach you how to use the Access Method Services (AMS) utility to define and manipulate VSAM files; and (2) to teach you how to process VSAM files using various programming languages. To be specific, you'll learn:

- how VSAM data sets and catalogs are organized and used

- how to use AMS commands to define VSAM catalogs, space, clusters, alternate indexes, and paths

- how to set AMS performance options so you make the best possible use of your system's resources

- what recovery and security considerations are important when you use AMS

- how to code MVS and DOS/VSE JCL for VSAM files, and how to allocate VSAM files under TSO and VM/CMS

- how to process VSAM files in COBOL, CICS, and assembler language (the chapter on COBOL processing covers both VS COBOL and VS COBOL II)

You'll find the answers to questions like these

- How much primary and secondary space should I allocate to my VSAM files?

- What's an appropriate free space allocation for a KSDS?

- What's the best control interval size for VSAM files that are accessed both sequentially and directly?

- Do I always need to use VERIFY to check the integrity of my files?

- What's the difference between regular VSAM catalogs and the ICF catalog structure?

- When should I...and shouldn't I...use the IMBED and REPLICATE options to improve performance?

- It's easy to find out how many records are in a file's index component. But how do I find out how many of those records are in the sequence set?

- How do I determine the best buffer allocation for my files?

- What's the best way to back up my VSAM files— REPRO, EXPORT, or something else?

So why wait any longer to sharpen your VSAM skills? Get a copy of *VSAM: AMS and Application Programming* TODAY!

VSAM: AMS & Application Programming,
12 chapters, 260 pages, **$27.50**
ISBN: 0-911625-33-X

VS COBOL II: A Guide for Programmers and Managers

Second Edition **Anne Prince**

This book builds on your COBOL knowledge to quickly teach you everything you need to know about VS COBOL II, the IBM 1995 COBOL compiler for MVS shops:

- how to code the new language elements...and what language elements you can't use any more

- CICS considerations

- how to use the new debugger

- how the compiler's features can make your programs compile and run more efficiently

- guidelines for converting to VS COBOL II (that includes coverage of the conversion aids IBM supplies)

So if you're in a shop that's already converted to VS COBOL II, you'll learn how to benefit from the new language elements and features the compiler has to offer. If you aren't yet working in VS COBOL II, you'll learn how to write programs now that will be easy to convert later on. And if you're a manager, you'll get some practical ideas on when to convert and how to do it as painlessly as possible.

This second edition covers Release 3 of the compiler, as well as Releases 1 and 2.

VS COBOL II, 7 chapters, 271 pages, **$27.50**
ISBN 0-911625-54-2

Structured ANS COBOL

A 2-part course in 1974 and 1985 ANS COBOL **Mike Murach and Paul Noll**

This 2-part course teaches how to use 1974 and 1985 standard COBOL the way the top professionals do. The two parts are independent: You can choose either or both, depending on your current level of COBOL skill (if you're learning on your own) or on what you want your programmers to learn (if you're a trainer or manager).

Part 1: A Course for Novices teaches people with no previous programming experience how to design and code COBOL programs that prepare reports. Because report programs often call subprograms, use COPY members, handle one-level tables, and read indexed files, it covers these subjects too. But frankly, this book emphasizes the structure and logic of report programs, instead of covering as many COBOL elements as other introductory texts do. That's because we've found most beginning programmers have more trouble with structure and logic than they do with COBOL itself.

Part 2: An Advanced Course also emphasizes program structure and logic, focusing on edit, update, and maintenance programs. But beyond that, it's a complete guide to the 1974 and 1985 elements that all COBOL programmers should know how to use (though many don't). To be specific, it teaches how to:

- handle sequential, indexed, and relative files

- use alternate indexing and dynamic processing for indexed files

- code internal sorts and merges

- create and use COPY library members

- create and call subprograms

- handle single- and multi-level tables using indexes as well as subscripts

- use INSPECT, STRING, and UNSTRING for character manipulation

- code 1974 programs that will be easy to convert when you switch to a 1985 compiler

In fact, we recommend you get a copy of *Part 2* no matter how much COBOL experience you've had because it makes such a handy reference to all the COBOL elements you'll ever want to use.

COBOL, Part 1, 13 chapters, 438 pages, **$32.50**
ISBN 0-911625-37-2

COBOL, Part 2, 12 chapters, 498 pages, **$32.50**
ISBN 0-911625-38-0

CICS for the COBOL Programmer

Second Edition

Doug Lowe

This 2-part course is designed to help COBOL programmers become outstanding CICS programs.

Part 1: An Introductory Course covers the basic CICS elements you'll use in just about every program you write. So you'll learn about basic mapping support (BMS), pseudo-conversational programming, basic CICS commands, sensible program design using event-driven design techniques, testing and debugging using IBM-supplied transactions (like CEMT, CECI, and CEDF) or a transaction dump, and efficiency considerations.

Part 2: An Advanced Course covers CICS features you'll use regularly, though you won't need all of them for every program. That means you'll learn about browse commands, temporary storage, transient data, data tables (including the shared data table feature of CICS 3.3), DB2 and DL/I processing considerations, distributed processing features,

interval control commands, BMS page building, and more! In addition, *Part 2* teaches you which features do similar things and when to use each one. So you won't just learn how to code new functions...you'll also learn how to choose the best CICS solution for each programming problem you face.

Both books cover all versions of CICS up through 3.3. Both cover OS/VS COBOL, VS COBOL II, and COBOL/370, so it doesn't matter which COBOL compiler you're using. And all the program examples in both books conform to CUA's Entry Model for screen design.

CICS, Part 1, 12 chapters, 409 pages, **$36.50**
ISBN 0-911625-60-7

CICS, Part 2, 12 chapters, 352 pages, **$36.50**
ISBN 0-911625-67-4

The CICS Programmer's Desk Reference

Second Edition

Doug Lowe

Ever feel buried by IBM manuals?

It seems like you need stacks of them, close at hand, if you want to be an effective CICS programmer. Because frankly, there's just too much you have to know to do your job well; you can't keep it all in your head.

That's why Doug Lowe decided to write *The CICS Programmer's Desk Reference*. In it, he's collected all the information you need to have at your fingertips, and organized it into 12 sections that make it easy for you to find what you're looking for. So there are sections on:

- BMS macro instructions—their formats (with an explanation of each parameter) and coding examples

- CICS commands—their syntax (with an explanation of each parameter), coding examples, and suggestions on how and when to use each one most effectively

- MVS and DOS/VSE JCL for CICS applications

- AMS commands for handling VSAM files

- details for MVS users on how to use ISPF

- complete model programs, including specs, design, and code

- a summary of CICS program design techniques that lead to simple, maintainable, and efficient programs

- guidelines for testing and debugging CICS applications

- and more!

So clear the IBM manuals off your terminal table. Let the *Desk Reference* be your everyday guide to CICS instead.

CICS Desk Reference, 12 sections, 507 pages, **$42.50**
ISBN 0-911625-68-2

 Call toll-free 1-800-221-5528 · Monday-Friday 8-5 Pacific Time · Fax: 1-209-275-9035

DB2 for the COBOL Programmer

Part 1: An Introductory Course   **Steve Eckols**

If you're looking for a practical DB2 book that focuses on application programming, this is the book for you. Written from the programmer's point of view, it will quickly teach you what you need to know to access and process DB2 data in your COBOL programs using embedded SQL. You'll learn:

- what DB2 is and how it works, so you'll have the background you need to program more easily and logically

- how to design and code application programs that retrieve and update DB2 data

- how to use basic error handling and data integrity techniques to protect DB2 data

- how to use joins and unions to combine data from two or more tables into a single table

- how to use DB2 column functions to extract summary information from a table

- how to use a subquery or subselect when one SQL statement depends on the results of another

- how to work with variable-length data and nulls

- how to develop DB2 programs interactively (using DB2I, a TSO facility) or in batch

So if you want to learn how to write DB2 application programs, get a copy of this book today!

DB2, Part 1, 11 chapters, 371 pages, **$36.50**
ISBN 0-911625-59-3

DB2 for the COBOL Programmer

Part 2: An Advanced Course   **Steve Eckols**

Once you've mastered the basics of DB2 programming, there's still plenty to learn. So this book teaches you all the advanced DB2 features that will make you a more capable programmer...and shows you when to use each one. You'll learn:

- how to use advanced data manipulation and error handling techniques

- how to use dynamic SQL

- how to work with distributed DB2 data

- how to maximize locking efficiency and concurrency to maintain the accuracy of DB2 data even while a number of programs have access to that data

- how to access and process DB2 data in CICS programs

- what you need to know about data base administration so you can design and define your own tables for program testing (this will make you a more productive and professional programmer, even if you never want to be a DBA)

- how to use QMF, IBM's Query Management Facility, to issue SQL statements interactively and to prepare formatted reports

So don't wait to expand your DB2 skills. Get a copy of this book TODAY.

DB2, Part 2, 15 chapters, 393 pages, **$36.50**
ISBN 0-911625-64-X

IMS for the COBOL Programmer

Part 1: DL/I Data Base Processing   **Steve Eckols**

This how-to book will have you writing batch DL/I programs in a minimum of time—whether you're working on a VSE or an MVS system. But it doesn't neglect the conceptual background you must have to create programs that work. So you'll learn:

- what a DL/I data base is and how its data elements are organized into a hierarchical structure

- the COBOL elements for creating, accessing, and updating DL/I data bases...including logical data bases and data bases with secondary indexing

- how to use DL/I recovery and restart features

- the basic DL/I considerations for coding interactive programs using IMS/DC or CICS

- how data bases with the 4 common types of DL/I data base organizations are stored (this material will help you program more logically and efficiently for the type of data base you're using)

- and more!

7 complete COBOL programs show you how to process DL/I data bases in various ways. Use them as models for production work in your shop, and you'll save hours of development time.

IMS, Part 1, 16 chapters, 333 pages, **$36.50**
ISBN 0-911625-29-1

IMS for the COBOL Programmer

Part 2: Data Communications and Message Format Service   **Steve Eckols**

The second part of *IMS for the COBOL Programmer* is for MVS programmers only. It teaches how to develop online programs that access IMS data bases and run under the data communications (DC) component of IMS. So you'll learn:

- why you code message processing programs (MPPs) the way you do (DC programs are called MPPs because they process messages sent from and to user terminals)

- what COBOL elements you use for MPPs

- how to use Message Format Service (MFS), a facility for formatting complex terminal displays so you can enhance the look and operation of your DC programs

- how to develop applications that use more than one screen format or that use physical and logical paging

- how to develop batch message processing (BMP) programs to update IMS data bases in batch even while they're being used by other programs

- how to use Batch Terminal Simulator (BTS) to test DC applications using IMS resources, but without disrupting the everyday IMS processing that's going on

- and more!

8 complete programs—including MFS format sets, program design, and COBOL code—show you how to handle various DC and MFS applications. Use them as models to save yourself hours of coding and debugging.

IMS, Part 2, 16 chapters, 398 pages, **$36.50**
ISBN 0-911625-30-5

MVS JCL

MVS/ESA • MVS/XA • MVS/370

Doug Lowe

Anyone who's worked in an MVS shop knows that JCL is tough to master. You learn enough to get by...but then you stick to that. It's just too frustrating to try to put together a job using the IBM manuals. And too time-consuming to keep asking your co-workers for help...especially since they're often limping along with the JCL they know, too.

That's why you need a copy of *MVS JCL*. It zeroes in on the JCL you need for everyday jobs...so you can learn to code significant job streams in a hurry.

You'll learn how to compile, link-edit, load, and execute programs. Process all types of data sets. Code JES2/JES3 control statements to manage job and program execution, data set allocation, and SYSOUT processing. Create and use JCL procedures. Execute general-purpose utility programs. And much more.

But that's not all this book does. Beyond teaching you JCL, it explains the basics of how MVS works so you can apply that understanding as you code JCL. You'll learn about the unique interrelationship between virtual storage and multiprogramming under MVS. You'll learn about data management: what data sets are and how data sets, volumes, and units are allocated. You'll learn about job management, including the crucial role played by JES2/JES3 as MVS processes jobs. And you'll learn about the components of a complete MVS system, including the role of system generation and initialization in tying the components together. That's the kind of perspective that's missing in other books and courses about MVS, even though it's background you must have if you want to bring MVS under your control.

MVS JCL, 17 chapters, 496 pages, **$42.50**
ISBN 0-911625-85-2

DOS/VSE JCL

Second Edition

Steve Eckols
The job control language for a DOS/VSE system can be overwhelming. There are more parameters than you would ever want to know about. And those parameters let you do more things than you would ever want to do. Of course, all those parameters are described in the IBM manuals...somewhere. But who has time to wade through pages and pages of details that don't seem to apply to your situation (although you can't ever be sure because the manuals are so confusing).

Certainly you don't. That's why you need *DOS/ VSE JCL*. It doesn't try to teach every nuance of every parameter. Instead, it teaches you how to code the JCL for the applications that occur every day in a VSE shop. You'll learn how to manage job and program execution, how to identify the files a program needs to use, and how to use cataloged procedures. You'll learn

how to code POWER JECL statements to manage job scheduling and output processing and how to use ICCF to manage POWER job processing. You'll learn how to process tape and DASD files. And you'll learn how to use language translators and the linkage-editor, maintain VSE libraries, and use three utility programs: sort/merge, DITTO, and AMS.

Whether you're a novice or an expert, this book will help you use your DOS/VSE system more effectively. If you're new to VSE, this book will get you started right, giving you the confidence you need to take charge of your system. If you're an experienced VSE user, this book will help you understand *why* you've been doing what you've been doing so you can do it better in the future.

DOS/VSE JCL, 18 chapters, 448 pages, **$34.50**
ISBN 0-911625-50-X

Comment form

Your opinions count

If you have comments, criticisms, or suggestions, I'm eager to get them. Your opinions today will affect our products of tomorrow. If you have questions, you can expect an answer within one week of the time we receive them. And if you discover any errors in this book, typographical or otherwise, please point them out so we can make corrections when the book is reprinted.

Thanks for your help.

Mike Murach
Fresno, California

Book title: VSAM for the COBOL Programmer (Second Edition)

_____
_____
_____
_____
_____
_____
_____
_____
_____
_____
_____
_____
_____
_____
_____
_____
_____
_____

Name & Title _____
Company (if company address) _____
Address _____
City, State, Zip _____

Fold where indicated and tape shut.
No postage necessary if mailed in the U.S.

fold

BUSINESS REPLY MAIL
FIRST-CLASS MAIL   PERMIT NO. 3063   FRESNO, CA

POSTAGE WILL BE PAID BY ADDRESSEE

Mike Murach & Associates, Inc.

4697 W JACQUELYN AVE
FRESNO CA 93722-9888

fold

fold

fold

Order Form

Our Unlimited Guarantee

To our customers who order directly from us: You must be satisfied. Our books must work for you, or you can send them back for a full refund...no questions asked.

Name & Title _____

Company (if company address) _____

Street address _____

City, State, Zip _____

Phone number (including area code) _____

Qty	Product code and title	*Price
VSAM		
___ VSMX	VSAM: Access Method Services and Application Programming	$27.50
___ VSMR	VSAM for the COBOL Programmer (Second Edition)	22.50
CICS		
___ CC1R	CICS for the COBOL Programmer Part 1 (Second Edition)	$36.50
___ CC2R	CICS for the COBOL Programmer Part 2 (Second Edition)	36.50
___ CRFR	The CICS Programmer's Desk Reference (Second Edition)	42.50
COBOL Language Elements		
___ VC2R	VS COBOL II (Second Edition)	$27.50
___ SC1R	Structured ANS COBOL, Part 1	32.50
___ SC2R	Structured ANS COBOL, Part 2	32.50
___ RW	Report Writer	17.50

Qty	Product code and title	*Price
Data Base Processing		
___ DB21	DB2 for the COBOL Programmer Part 1: An Introductory Course	$36.50
___ DB22	DB2 for the COBOL Programmer Part 2: An Advanced Course	36.50
___ IMS1	IMS for the COBOL Programmer Part 1: DL/I Data Base Processing	36.50
___ IMS2	IMS for the COBOL Programmer Part 2: Data Communications and MFS	36.50
MVS Subjects		
___ MJLR	MVS JCL (Second Edition)	$42.50
___ TSO1	MVS TSO, Part 1: Concepts and ISPF	36.50
___ TSO2	MVS TSO, Part 2: Commands and Procedures (CLIST and REXX)	36.50
___ MBAL	MVS Assembler Language	36.50
DOS/VSE Subjects		
___ VJLR	DOS/VSE JCL (Second Edition)	$34.50
___ ICCF	DOS/VSE ICCF	31.00
___ VBAL	DOS/VSE Assembler Language	36.50

☐ Bill me for the books plus UPS shipping and handling (and sales tax within California).

☐ Bill my company. P.O.#_____

☐ I want to **SAVE 10%** by paying in advance. Charge to my
____Visa ____MasterCard ____American Express:
Card number _____
Valid thru (mo/yr) _____
Cardowner's signature _____

☐ I want to **SAVE 10% plus shipping and handling**. Here's my check or money order for the books minus 10% ($_____). California residents, please add sales tax to your total. (Offer valid in U.S.)

* Prices are subject to change. **Please call for current prices.**

To order more quickly,

Call **toll-free** 1-800-221-5528

(Weekdays, 8 to 5 Pacific Time)

Fax: 1-209-275-9035

Mike Murach & Associates, Inc.

2560 West Shaw Lane, Suite 101
Fresno, California 93711-2765
(209) 275-3335